Dedicated to My Guru Dada USTAD MUSHTAQ ALI KHAN

INDIAN CLASSICAL MUSIC

AND

SENIA GHARANA'S CONTRIBUTION

(With a life sketch of MIAN TANSEN)

Sunita Dhar

RELIANCE PUBLISHING HOUSE

NEW DELHI

1995 Edition

ISBN: 81-85047-49-9

Published by:
S.K. Bhatia *for*
Reliance Publishing House
3026/7H, Ranjit Nagar,
New Delhi-110008.
Ph. 5722605

Composed by:
Geeta Graphics
3026/7H, Ranjit Nagar,
New Delhi-110008

Printed at Excellent Printers, B-85
Naraina Industrial Area, New Delhi.

FOREWORD

The study of Indian Music has become subject of Study in Universities in India today. More people have come forward to study and have research on the subject in order to find out the past with logical references.

There have been many attempts to place the genealogical history of TANSEN, the father of Indian Music, on record but none of those attempts finally reached a destination. The family trees of the Great Master is still a matter of debate, so far his ancestors are concerned. Mrs. Sunita Dhar has tried to bring not only the history of the family, collecting informations from various reliable sources, but also tried to document certain compositions. There has been a long felt need for a compendium of information about MIAN TANSEN and Mrs. Dhar has made an attempt with utmost zeal and sincerity.

Although such work can not be complete because of the absence of any document and the only dependable source is the living legends of Indian Music. Mrs. Sunita Dhar, being my student, I have a great pleasure to introduce this work as an attempt to bring out the hidden facts on the Great Master TANSEN. Many of the facts during TANSEN's time have become a story today. Such a Maestro's work can not be complete and the future generation will try to find out more facts in order to bring out a new dimension on the life of this Great Master.

I am conscious of the deficiencies which is bound to be there in such a reference work in the absence of any logical document. Many scholars are coming forward and many will come, and I am sure this work will certainly supplement the effort of the future scholars who would like to have a further research on GREAT MIAN TANSEN.

I am sure, the readers will immensely be benefited with the references and compositions of the Great Master. I will be extremely happy if this work helps the future generation to know and learn about the Father of Indian Music MIAN TANSEN. Being a SENIA (a follower of TANSEN) myself, I feel happy to wish this publication a good future.

PROF. DEBU CHAUDHURI
Former Dean, Faculty of Music & Fine Arts, University of Delhi.

New Delhi
March 15, 1989

CONTENTS

ACKNOWLEDGEMENTS

My Guru Professor Debu Chaudhuri has been a beacon light for me since my days as a student in the Delhi University. He spotted and fomented my aptitude for music and fostered it for research. My academic pursuit to prepare this work got goaded by his apt suggestion as my guide, "Senia Gharana and its contribution to Indian Classical Music", as the topic for my work. My labours in this direction got nourished and sustained by his sympathetic and sweet encouragements in sessions of discussions we had on various points from time to time. I am greatly indebted to him.

The abundant and valuable assistance that I enjoyed from Dr. (Mrs.) Sumati Mutatkar, Ex-Dean of Faculty of Music & Fine Arts, University of Delhi, gave me an immense comfort at various stages of my work. I am very thankful to her for her help, suggestions and constant encouragement throughout the investigations.

My Guru Dada Ustad Mushtaq Ali Khan of the Senia Gharana was warmly helpful and made me feel perfectly at home in new surroundings. I collected very helpful and relevant information by personal interviews and communications regarding various items from him. This could not, however, be pursued without his help. I express my gratitude to him for such a guidance.

I also collected very helpful and relevant information by personal interviews and communications regarding various items from the following old masters & musicians of Senia Gharana, Late Shri Birendra Kishore Roy Chaudhuri, Late Shri Bimal Kant Roy Choudhuri, Prof. D.T. Joshi, Late Professor Radhika Mohan. Pandit Ravi Shankar, Ustad Illyas Khan, Ustad Asad Ali Khan

(Beenkar); Shri Dalip Chander Bedi, Shri Nikhil Banerjee and Dr. Sharmistha Sen.

Finally I am grateful to my father-in-law Professor Ved Lal Dhar who provided me all possible help and support in the completion and submission of this thesis.

INTRODUCTION

Music enlightens the soul and broadens human intellect, helping attainment of 'BRAHMAGYANA'. It has universal appeal and has been used as medium to convey the deepest of human emotions, in all moods from spiritual ecstacy, to love. It's love is not only prerogative of humans from richest of kings to poorest of peasants but birds and beasts like it and even plants are said to respond to it.

Origin of Indian music is unclear. It is closely linked to religion and hence to Gods and Goddesses, *Rishis* and *Munis*. From Vedic times when it existed as hymns it developed into classical form due to adoption of various innovations. Earliest documentation is found in NATYASHASTRA of BHARATA. Indian music has scientific basis. Its growth has been organised and systematic, being enriched by various influences yet maintaining its vigour and popularity, without losing its identity for thousands of years before christ to present day.

In music as in any art form there is harmonious blending of ideas and techniques. In medieval times Indian Music has had patronage from Hindu Rajas and various invading victors. This helped to the rise of *Bhakti* Movement and *Sufism* Yet Hindustani music has retained its rich Indian tradition and its interaction with influences other than Indian.

In Mughal days appreciation, patronage and recognition helped in the growth of Indian Music. Akbar's reign has become immortalised in the history of Hindustani Music because of the presence of great musicians like Tansen. Great attention was given by the Emperor to music. Many instrumentalists specialising in various instruments, contributed to the popularity of music. The musicians belonged to different religions and regions. They came from diverse castes and social backgrounds. Only Love of music was common in them.

In Akbar's time temple culture of music and dance was revived. Predominant place was given to *Dhrupada* in the sphere of classical music. A list of musicians includes Mian Tansen, Sujan Khan, Baba Ramdas, Baj Bahadur, Bilas Khan, Tan-Tarang and Surdas son of Ramdas and others.

A legacy of that time has descended to this day, which has preserved the tradition of that time upto now. Music has an artistic side, and a scientific aspect as well. It has its own rules and laws. In it every note and melody has mathematical formulae. In order to master the art of music one has to devote many years to its practice. It requires patience and diligence. Besides this, another important factor is that it has a tradition. In Indian music there are rich traditions. They have sustained the sublimity of Indian music and also have heightened its role in life. Our music has developed from past to present on the basis of traditions or instructions from generation to generation. The value of tradition in Indian music may be judged from the fact that every aspirant could not learn music as there were no facilities of text books and paid *Ustads* then. Some aspirants with rich voice and talent or with nimble fingers, possessing perseverance could win their maestro's favour by their singular devotion. All instructions were imparted only by the *Gurus* to the disciples at their houses. This relationship between *Guru* and disciple has a sort of sanctity and affectional disposition from one towards the other. The instructions and lessons spread over a long period of time and required discipline of mind and the body. Such musicians could develop their own musical forms, which gave rise to new traditions in classical music, as the disciple musicians practised for long hours over a long period of time and thus developed super conciousness of musical notes and melodies and also acquired the ability to create new musical forms by the invocation of their own creativity and imagination.

In Akbar's time Tansen enriched classical music by discovering many ragas and by many innovations in Indian Classical Music. He did a lot of work for the improvement of music in his days. That legacy in music is perpetuated even to this day by some of the musicians. Such *Ustads* either directly or indirectly, Vocalist or instrumentalist, are linked with Tansen's *Gharana*

The study we have undertaken is concerned with highlighting the creative contributions to Classical Music, Vocal and Instrumental, made by the musicians belonging to *Senia Gharana*, the origin of which starts from Tansen.

In *Senia Gharana* we find instances of such creative genius amongst some musicians. An intensive study has been made to identify the innovations, modifications, improvisations, as well as creations of *Ragas* musical forms and musical compositions and the instrumental techniques by the *Senia Gharana*

The *Senia Gharana* is one which has strictly followed teachings of Mian Tansen through his disciples and descendants in Vocal & Instrumental music having enriched, modified and invented new styles.

In *Senia Gharana* the first and the foremost contributions towards Indian Classical Music is done by the sons and the daughter of Tansen. They developed the *Dhrupada* form of music with certain distinct melodies. They used to sing *Dhrupada* in a pure and melodious way, with *meends* in straight lines according to the structure of the *Ragas* Some of their *Dhrupadas* are still available. Bilas Khan, the Chief Court Musician of Jehangir (1605-1627), was a specialist in the *Dhrupada* of *Shuddha Vani* . *Raga Bilaskhani Todi* was invented by Bilas Khan which is very famous today. Lal Khan the son-in-law of Bilas Khan got the title of *"Gun Samundhar"* in 1630 from Emperor Shah Jehan for the development of classical music. His style of singing resembled Tansen's singing. Khushal Khan being an accomplished musician of Dhrupada was given the title of *"Gun Samundhar"* by Aurangzeb. Many of his Dhrupada's are still available and are given in Chapter four.

Senias were masters of Vocal Music as well as instrumental such as *Been* etc. *Been* was in existence in *Vedic* times under different names and forms such as, *Tata, Vitata, Vana* , Maha Veena, *Shatatantu* etc. During Tansen's period *Been* gained much popularity. Tansen's daughter and her husband, Misri Singh, formed the main *Gharana* of *Been* Senias produced the intricate embellishments of the Vocal *Alap in Veena*. Being a master in *Dhrupada* form of music, Niyamat Khan is credited to have made *Been* a solo instrument.

Rabab was a popular folk instrument of North India. Senia's made it a stylized classical instrument. By their creativity it gained tremendous popularity. Tansen and his disciples are credited for raising it to the status of a classical instrument. Some musicologists hold Tansen as its innovater. Bahadur Sen of *Senia Gharana* introduced many new *alankars* in Rabab. The technique of instrument Rabab is described in the concluding page of Chapter five.

Another contribution of *Senia Gharana* towards Indian Classical Music is the development of *Khayal* style. *Khayal* was already in existence mostly in *Khairabadi* language. Niyamat Khan, in the line of Tansen's daughter, is credited to have given a new turn to it. The mystic elements in Khayal were substituted by artistic and aesthetic features by him. Niyamat Khan endeavoured to incorporate the characteristics of *Dhrupada* into *Khayal* in which he became successful. His compositions in *Khayal* acquired such popularity that even today the musicians recite them, and use them as a model for new compositions shown in Chapter seventh.

Sur-Sringar was invented by Jafar Khan a descendant of Tansen. This instrument is like *Sur-Bahar* and both these instruments were made for *Alap* by *Senias*. *Sur-Bahar* was introduced by Ghulam Muhammad Khan, a student of Pyar Khan of *Senia Gharana*.

The last but not the least, contribution of Senia *Gharana* is towards Sitar, described in Chapter eighth. Sitar was already in existence under the name of Seh Tar, *Tritantri* etc. Sitar was of three strings. Amrit Sen introduced more strings *to* it and advocated the use of 17 frets in the Sitar. The tunning system also was introduced by Senias. Maseet Khan innovated the *Maseetkhani Baj* in Sitar which is famous even today. Senias are credited to have brought Sitar to the level of *Been* They introduced elements of Veena, *Dhrupada* and *Khayal* n Sitar. They are credited to have introduced greater use of *Meend* and *Layakari* n *Masitkhani Baj*. The contributions of Senia musicians in Sitar upto now have been briefly summarised in the last Chapter.

With the passage of time, the *Senia Gharana*'s specialities in various fields of music have been or are heading towards vanishing point, except in Sitar. In *Dhrupada Been Rabab Sur-Sringar* new styles or specialities, deviating from Senia traditions are in vogue. But in Sitar Senia traditions are sustained and also enriched by some of the musicians such as Ustad Mushtaq Ali Khan, Pandit Ravi Shankar, Prof. Debu Chaudhuri, Shri Nikhil Banerjee, Shri Rameshwar Pathak, Ustad Illyas Khan etc.

CHAPTER I

GHARANA

The word *Gharana* has evolved from the Sanskrit word *Griha* (Home), from which Hindi word *Ghar* (Home) seems to have been derived. The word *Gharana* means family relations of blood connections having common heritage, caste or living under the same roof. Upkeeping family prestige, name, fame and glory are characteristics of a family. In simple words, it is, more or less, the members of a joint family which can be called a *Gharana*, who leave behind, after death, their specialities and particularities for their generations to follow.

In terminology of music *Gharana* has acquired a meaning which denotes the direct descendants of a master musician, who have received training under him and have imbibed the peculiar characteristics of the style of musical delineation of the master. *Gharana* is established and accepted as such only when its adherents, descendants, and followers keep up the traditional lineage in respect of the peculiarities of its style and technique and, as such, when a duration of atleast three generations possess a *Gharana* is established. *Gharana* can also be defined as a particular style of music preserved by the master musicians from time to time and even added to, to beautify its charm and speciality.

Starting back from Emperor *Akbar's* time till the first quarter of the 20th Century, Hindustani Music is specially linked with the *Dhrupada* tradition of *Tansen* and the *Khayal* tradition of *Qawwals* and *Kalawants*. The music of this period is known as modern Hindustani Music which is completely linked with *Gharana* system. Musicians followed the *Gharana* system during this period. *Gharana* system in music during this period also came to be known as *Taksali Sangit*, because of its value of purity and standard; as coins produced in Mint (*Taksal*) can not be impure and below standard, so also the music produced and preserved by *Gharanas*, is pure and of high standard.[1]

According to Prof. Radhika Mohan Moitra,[2] the range of music has sufficiently been widened by musicians of different *Gharanas* as per their tradition and style of putting forward *Dhrupada*, *Damar*, *Khayal*, *Tappa*, *Tarana* etc., in different way, so as to produce different kinds of tastes and pleasure to the listeners.

In no other branch of man's thinking, imagination, literature, painting, sculpture and other fine arts, this particular term, *Gharana*, is used except in Hindustani Music. This is a special kind of characteristic of Hindustani Music only. *Gharana*, as it is extant today, existed in ancient times perhaps in the different forms in music and in different fields. We find various names like *Samhitas*, *Shakhas*, *Naradi Shiksha*, *Guru Shishya Parampara*, *Sampradaya*, *Muttas*, *Giti* and *Vani* etc., for different traditions of music followers at different times in the history of Hindustani Music. Therefore, it becomes necessary here to trace the history and evolution of *Gharana*.

Going back to *Vedic* times, the *Vedic* hymns can be regarded as India's most ancient music. These hymns needed clear enunciation and emphasis on particular syllables and words, some long drawn and some with short intermittent breaks, which were produced through proper modulation of the voice. This gave rise to a class of priest singers, and essentials of both, melody and rhythm, came into prominence. The musical rendering of each hymn basically differed in respect to the number of Svaras used with the method of singing. This provided the nucleus for different styles of chants and singing which developed into various *Shakhas* (branches) or *Samhita*.[3]

In early times *Sam-Vedic* Brahmins formulated certain

---

1. Chobey, Sushel Kumar - Sangit Ke Gharano Ke Charcha, p. 12.
2. Personal communications with Prof. Radhika Mohan Moitra.
3. Dr. Winternetz. - 'A History of Indian Literature', Part I, pp. 53-56.

rules for singing which were handed down by oral tradition and were in turn incorporated in the *Samanas* as *Gramageya* and *Araneyageya*.[1] The system of giving oral lessons in *Vedic* chants continued upto 1000 B.C.[3]

During the period 600-500 B.C., we find reference to four main schools of Music, Dance and Drama. These schools were termed as *Sampradayas* and were classified as follows:-

I. Brahmabharta:-- The School of *BRAHMA AND SADASIVA* - Bharta or the school of Shiva

II. The School of *GANDHARVA NARADA*.

III. The School of *MUNI BHARATA*.

IV. The School of *NANDIKESWARA*.

Some are of the opinion that there were only three schools, such as:--

I. The *Natya-Sampradaya* of Bharata.

II. The *Nardiya Ghandharva* Sampradaya.

III. The *Nandikeswara* Sampradaya.[3]

There is however, a reference to Brahma's *Mata* in Matanga's Brahaddesi which had been quoted by Bharata,[4] which shows that four schools existed during this time.

During this period reference is also found in Chinese annals regarding family traditions. During 577-550 B.C. some Brahmin musician families went over to China and were called *TSAO* by the Chinese. Remarkable representative of this family was Mia-Ta. Sujiva came to the Chinese Court between 573-560 B.C. He is reported to have said that his father, who was famous as a musician, had learnt music through a tradition transmitted through generations.[5]

Bharta Muni and Nandikeswara established their

---

1. Dr. Caland, 'Introduction to Panchavimsha Brahman,Chapter II, p. 13.
2. Macdonell, A., 'India's Past - A Survey of her Literature Religions Languages and Antiquities', p. 51.
3. Prajanananda, Swami - 'History of Indian Music.', Part I, p. 11.
4. Matanga Muni - The Brahaddesi, p. 370.
5. Bagchi P.C. 'India and China', 2nd Ed., p. 167.

schools on dance and dramaturgy in the second & fifth Century A.D. respectively.[1] The followers of Bharta Muni in dramaturgy were called *Bharatas*. Nandikeswara recognised a class of Murchhana consisting of twelve notes. Murchhana was a closely guarded secret of the Acharyas (Guru), which they passed on to their direct descendants. Even then, occasionally a very close disciple could earn the favour of his teacher through hard work and devotion and the Guru passed on this secret to his pupil without making any distinction between him and his son. This is the beginning of what is known as (*Guru-Shishya-Parampara*).[2]

During 2nd half of the 15th Century, Kallinatha made a brief mention of *Sampradaya* while discussing *Grama Jati* and *Murchhana* The word *Sampradaya* signifies a school of thought.[3] *Sampradayas*, in due course, have given rise to different *Matas* or schools which developed on the same basic concepts and acquired the names of their originators.

The main *Matas* were:-

1. SIVA MATA;
2. KRISHNA MATA;
3. HANUMAN MATA;
4. BHARATA MATA;
5. KALLINATHA MATA.

Pandit Damodar, in 16th Century A.D., only has written on the dramatic aspects of music but also threw some light on different *MATA* or schools of thought which were in vogue in his time.[4]

The next phase in the process of development was reached with the emergence of *Geetis*. In Natya-Shastra (2nd Century), we find mention of four kinds of *Geetis* In Brahaddesi (6th Century), we find only a brief description of *Prabandhas* but in Manasollasa (early 12th Century), Sangita Samayasara (Late 12th Century) and Sangita Ratnakara (13th Century), we find that *Prabandhas* have

---

1. Krishna, Mangesh Ram, 'Sangita Makaranda of Narada', p. 10, Introduction.
2. Sharang Deva, 'Sangit Ratnakara, Vol.I, p. 108.
3. Sharang Deva, Sangit Ratnakara', Vol. I, p. 108.
4. Damodar, Chatur- 'Sangit Darpan'.

been dealt with elaborately while there is no mention of *Dhruvas* (stage songs). By this time *Prabandhas* had gained wide popularity and *Dhruvas* became obsolete. By about the 15th Century, when the Prabandhas became for too stereotyped and effete, a simplified derivation of it emerged in the form of *Dhrupada*

In *Dhrupada* we find the name of four different Vanis which were based on four or five gitis and which indicate four different styles of *Dhrupad* as follows:-

1. *Goudhari Vani*,
2. *Dagar Vani*.,[2]
3. *Nauhari Vani*,[3]
4. *Shudda Vani*[1].

These four *Vanis* are derived from the four types of *Svarasrita-Gitis*. There is controversy as to which Giti gave birth to which *Vani* It is felt that *Shuddha Vani* is derived from *Sadharani Giti*, Godhari Vani from Gaudi Giti, *Khandari Vani* from *Bhinna Giti*, *Dagore Vani* from *Suddha Giti* and *Nauhara Vani* from *Veswara Giti*.[4]

According to Shri Birendra Kishore Roy Chaudhuri, Goudhar Vani is derived from *Shastrik Shuddha Giti*, *Dagore Vani* is derived from *Bhinna Giti*, *Khandari Vani* is derived from *Beswara Giti*, *Nauhari Vani* is derived from *Goudi Giti*. The two authors however are controversial as to which *Giti* gave birth to which *Vani*. Also the latter is silent about the fifth *Vani*.

The second view as to the origin of *Vanis* holds that the *Vanis* derived their names from the places where they developed and flourished. In a famous song beginning with the "*"Pada Vani Charoki Bayohar Suno Ligiea"*", composed by Mian Tansen, the merits of these four *Vanis* have been discussed. In this song he stated that the king of all *Vanis* was *Goudhar* The *Khandhar* was the general. The Minister was *Dagore* and *Nauhar* was the menial officer. Although Tansen gave first place to *Goudhar Vani*, he admitted the

1. Srivastava, Indurama-"Dhrupada", p. 8.
2. Prajanananda, Swami, 'A History of Indian Music', p. 185-86
3. Roy Chaudhuri Birendra Kishore, 'Indian Music & Mian Tansen', p. 7.
4. Srivastava, Indurama 'Dhrupada', p. 8.

neccessity of all the four *Vanis* and placed them in their proper status.

After the end of the Mughal empire, we find the growth of some famous *Gharanas*, each specialising in singing in some of the four *Vanis* of Dhrupada. Thus each style of singing *Dhrupada*, in one or more *Vanis*, which was known at that time as *Vani*, gave rise to *Gharanas*. Here it becomes necessary for us to trace the history of association of *Vanis* with different *Gharanas* and how different *Gharanas* were established.

Mian Tansen was the greatest disciple of Swami Haridasa. The other notable disciples of Swami Haridasa were Brij Chand, Gopal Lal, Maharaja Samokhan Singh of Ajmer. From the period of Akbar, notable *Gharanas* of Northern Indian were formed by the descendants or disciples of above mentioned musicians. Mian Tansen was accepted as the greatest of all musicians by Emperor Akbar. His influence on other musicians was paramount. He formed the main *Gharana*, that is, the *Senia Gharana* of Hindustani Music.

According to Muhammad Karam Imam,[1] *Gobarhara Vani* is said to have been introduced by Tansen. It is so called because Tansen was a *Goudiya Brahmin*. The other reason for the name is given because Tansen developed it in Gwalior, the dialect of that place was known as *Gobarhara*. Through a process of linguistic distortion, *Gopahari* became *Gobarhari*.[2] The third reason is that this *Vani* is named after a place near Gwalior where from Tansen was supposed to have come.[3] The peculiarity of Goudhar Vani is that in it are incorporated many of the old musical touches. It evokes *Santa Rasa* or serentiy of the mind. Its gait is slow or elephantine.[4]

According to descendants of Tansen it is sung in a pure and melodious way containing *MEENDS*, in straight lines, according to the structure of the *Ragas* Mian Tansen

---

1. Imam, Karam Hakim - Madunul Mausiqui, pp. 23-24.
2. Brahaspati K.D. 'Dhrupad Aur Uska Vikas, pp. 276-77.
3. Dvivedi, 'Gwalior Ke Tomartha', p. 296
4. Goswami O, 'The Story of Indian Music, p. 125.
5. Interviews with Shri Birendra Kishore Roy Chaudhuri.

himself was a master of this style as well and in the line of his youngest son, Bilas Khan, this style was mainly used. Bilas Khan formed first *Seni Gharana* at Delhi Darbar. Celebrated descendants who followed this *vani* were Pyar Khan, Jaffar Khan, Basat Khan. They used to play on Rabab and sing *Dhrupada's*.[1]

The *Dagar Vani* which is supposed to have been introduced by Brij Chand, originated in *DAGARA* which was near Delhi and is presently known as Danga,[2] while it is also said that the style was introduced by Brij Chand in Rajputana.[3] Brij Chand was conferred the title of Chand Khan by Akbar and was a Brahman of Dagur near Delhi.[4] The *Goudi* style of singing *Dhrupada* - is slow and heavy in movement and requires great control of breath. In its execution, it is rigid and disciplined. It is marked by correct intonation, purity of design, simplicity of execution and massiveness of structure. Occasionally when it was sung at medium speed and there was a judicious blending with it of the *Khandar* style to add colour to the performance, it was called *Dagar Vani*.[5] The *Dagar Vani* aroused sentimental appeal and soft passion by using *Meends* & *Alankars*. This *Vani* resembles the ancient *Binna Giti* which specialises in delicately executed *Meends* with *Gamakas*. This vani is said to have been popularised by the disciples of *Swami Haridasa*. The descendants of Misri Singh also took to this *Vani*, since we find a number of *Dagar Vani Dhrupadas* in the repertoire of descendants of Misri Singh, who married Saraswati Devi, the daughter of Tansen. This style was mainly adopted by Surat Sen, who was the son of Tansen. His descendants subsequently settled at Jaipur.[6]

Khandari Vani is supposed to have been introduced by Samokhan Singh and originated in *Khandara-Pradesha*

---

1. Roy Chaudhuri Birendra Kishore, 'Indian Music & Mian Tansen', p. 7.
2. Brahaspati K.D., 'Dhrupad Aur Uska Vikas', p. 277.
3. Goswami O, 'The Story of Indian Music', p. 126.
4. Imam, Karam Hakim, Madunul Mausiqui, pp. 23-24.
5. Goswami O,'The Story of Indian Music', p. 126.
6. Roy Chaudhuri Birendra Kishore, 'Indian Music & Mian Tansen', p. 27.

(Rajasthan), the dialect of which is known as Khandari.[1] Samokhan Singh, a *Beenkar* of great repute, married to daughter of Tansen and was given the title of Naubat Khan by Akbar.[2] However, as per the literature available, it is said that Misri Singh son of Samokhan Singh, who was Tansen's son-in-law, got the title of Naubat Khan from Akbar. *Khandari Vani* was originated by Samokhan Singh, and later Naubat Khan popularised it. The *Khandari Vani* is rich in variety and resembles the old *Vesara* or *Vegaswara Geeti*. Its gait is majestic and it uses heavy and vigorous style, expressive of valour. In this style the song is sung in pieces as on *Veena*. This is the most representative style. Its speciality is its capacity to create variety and it is full of richness. It evokes the *Tivra Rasa*, or feeling of exhilaration in the mind. In marked contrast to the *Goudi* style, it is never sung in very slow rhythm, and it is forceful and full of movement. But it certainly does not involve the tonal acrobatics that are associated with it now-a-days. This style was mainly adopted by Misri Singh and his descendants formed the main *Gharana* of *Veena* music and used to sing *Dhrupada* in both *Dagar* & *Khandari vani* This line of *Gharana* is also known as *Senia Gharana* because of marriage of Misri Singh with Tansen's daughter.[3] *Nauhar Vani* is said to have been introduced by Sri Chand, and originated in a place called Nauhar in the Delhi Province.[4] Muhammad Karam Imam writes that Sri Chand was a Rajput of Nooha district in Rajasthan, a disciple of Swami Haridasa. He joined the Court of Akbar and received the title of Suraj Khan from the emperor.[5] The *Nauhar Vani* resembles the *Goudi giti* which has an abundance of *Chhut-tanas*. It is characterised by quick, jerky passages employing a veriety of *Gamakas* It usually moves in quick succession, moving as it were in slow curved lines accompanied by the judicious use of soft *Gamakas* from the first to its third or fourth notes and evokes what is

---

1. Srivastava Indurama, 'Dhrupada', p. 50.
2. Imam, Hakim Karam, 'Madunul Mausiqui' pp. 23-24.
3. Based on Interview with Shri Birendra Kishore Roy Chaudhuri, Calcutta.
4. Goswami, O, 'The Story of Indian Music', p. 124.
5. Imam, Hakim Karam, 'Modunul Mausiqui', pp. 23-24 & 233.

known as *Adbhuta Rasa*.[1] It seems all musicians used *Nauhar Vani* as a variation.

After the death of Tansen all descendants of Tansen are now known as *Senia's*. As per the Genealogical Chart (in Chapter 3), we can trace the line of Bilas Khan and Misri Singh to present day musicians. The lines of other sons of Tansen are not traceable. The line of Surat Sen who settled at Jaipur, has Mohan Sen as descendant of Surat Sen and Sudhin Sen as descendant of Mohan Sen. Subsequently, it seems, his line vanished or the musicians of his line merged with the musicians of other two lines. The Seni Gharana of Sitar of Jaipur as known now-a-days, was subsequently founded by the celebrated Masit Sen, Rahim Sen and Amrit Sen who were the descendants of Bilas Khan.[2] In Instrumental Music the descendants of Bilas Khan took to Rabab playing, whereas the descendant of Tansen's daughter's line popularised the Veena in instruments.[3]

Some orthodox musicians are of the opinion that *Khandar Vani* developed by Raja Samokhan Singh, has been specially devised for the *Veena*.[4] *Goudi Vani* is suitable for the Rabab and the *Sur-Sringara*, *Dagar Vani* for the Sitar and *Nauhar Vani* for the Sarod. Different *Vani's* are suitable for different instruments according to their limitations. Generally the *Vanis* are utilised in the Alap portion. In the slow movement of Alap, *Goudari Vani* and *Dagar Vani* are applied. Gradually, as the speed increases, the *Khandari* and *Nauhar Vani's* are used.

Besides these *Gharanas*, we find the name of Agra *Gharana* specialising in Dhamar style formed by Haji Sujan Khan, which was famous during the reign of Emperor Shah Jehan A.D. (1625-1658). In A.D. 1658 Shah Jehan's, third son Aurangzeb (Reign A.D. 1658-1707) imprisoned his father, murdered his brothers and became the emperor. He was famous for his hatredness of music, during his time the Classical Music declined, musicians of all the *Gharanas* underwent severe hardships. After

1. Interview with Shri Birendra Kishore Roy Chaudhuri, Calcutta.
2. Interview with Shri Birendra Kishore Roy Chaudhuri.
3. Imam, Hakim Karam, 'Madunul Mausiqui', p. 24.
4. Based on Interview with Shri Radhika Mohan Moitra.

Aurangzeb his son Bahadur Shah, (Reign A.D. 1707-1712), ascended the throne. The great musician Niyamat Khan (Sadarang) from Tansen's daughter's line, was his court musician. From A.D. 1712 to 1719, four kings ruled but subsequently Muhammed Shah Rangeelay (Reign A.D. 1719-1748) ascended the throne. He earned the title Rangeelay, meaning (colourful) because of his colourful personality and his love for easy life. He was great lover of music and it is during his reign that Delhi *Darbar* was revived with musicians of all *Gharanas* assembling at Delhi.[1] Niyamat Khan was the high priest of Muhammad Shah's Darbar and is ranked as the second great Musician of India after Mian Tansen. He invented the new technique of Veena music and Dhamar. He also created the classical *Khayal* and founded the famous Qawwal *Gharana* through his disciples, whom he taught classical *Khayal*. The Qawwal *Gharana* thus formed was regarded as the authoritative line of *Khayal*. Other *Gharanas* like Agra *Gharana* and Gwalior *Gharana* of *Khayal* grew up from the main Qawwal *Gharana*.[2] After Niyamat Khan, in 20th Century, there evolved some colourful novel styles in Khayal through individual efforts-cum-methods of execution or embellishment and they were named after noted places (Seats of Culture) and artists. To name a few, Gwalior *Gharana*, Agra *Gharana*, Jaipur *Gharana*, Patiala *Gharana*, Kirana *Gharana*, Alladiya Khan *Gharana* etc. Different kinds of *Gamakas*, subtle tana, *Meends*, Vani, Laya, Tempo etc. were the salient features consisting their differences.[3]

During the middle of the 18th Century, the main *Gharanas* of Hindustani Music which were founded by the Seni Musicians and their disciples took final shape. The main Gharanas were as follows :-

1. Seni *Gharana* of Dhrupada and Rabab, formed by three great brothers, Jafar Khan, Pyar Khan & Basat Khan of Lucknow and Banaras.
2. Seni *Veenkaras* laid by Nirmal Shah of Lucknow.

---

1. Srivastava, Indurama, 'Dhrupada', p. 25.
2. Roy Chaudhuri, Birendra Kishore, 'Indian Music & Mian Tansen', p. 28.
3. Prajanananda, Swami, 'A Historical Survey of Indian Music', p. 215.

3. Qawwal *Gharana* laid by Bade Muhammad Khan Qawwal of Lucknow and Gwalior.
4. Gwalior *Gharana* of Khayal formed by the three great Khayali brothers Haddu Khan, Hassu Khan & Nathu Khan.
5. Agra *Gharana* of Khayal and Dhamar formed by the descendants of Hazi Sujan Khan (Dhamar) and who later on became disciples of Shah Sadarang.
6. Betia *Gharana* of Dhrupada formed by the disciples of Haidar Khan Seni of Lucknow, who were the *Kathakas* of Banaras, as well as Muslim Ustads of Kalpi.
7. Bishnupur *Gharana* of Dhrupada, formed by Bahadur Khan Seni, through his disciple Ram Shankar Bhattacharjee.
8. Tilmandi *Gharana* of Punjabi Dhrupada singers.
9. Lahore *Gharana* by Punjabi Khayalias, disciples of Sadarang.
10. Ataruli *Gharana* of Dhrupad & Khayal founded by the Brahmins of Mathura who embraced Islam later on.
11. Dagar *Gharana*, founded by Bairam Khan, a great scholar and Dhrupad singer, who was a descendant of a priestly line of Mathura.
12. The Seni *Gharana* of Sitar of Jaipur founded by the celebrated Amrit Sen.
13. The Sarod *Gharana* of Saharanpur, disciples of Omrao Khan, a son of Nirmal Shah Seni.
14. Sarod *Gharana* founded by Niamatullah Khan, a disciple of Basat Khan Seni.
15. The Sitar *Gharana* of Lucknow founded by Gulam Muhammad or Raza Khan, a disciple of Omrao Khan Seni.[1]

Further mention can be made about the Rampur *Gharana* which is latest and the last of the greatest *Gharanas* of India.

After the end of the Sepoy Mutiny, Wazed Ali Shah, the great patron of music settled at Calcutta after having come

1. Roy Chaudhuri, Birendra Kishore, 'Indian Music & Mian Tansen', p. 30.

from Lucknow. He brought with him the great musicians like Basat Khan, Kasem Ali Mian of the Tansen's line and Murad Ali Khan and Taj Khan of Kulpi School and some outstanding *Khayalias* also.

Among the other great musicians of the Tansen line Sadeque Ali Khan, the great Rababi and scholar settled in Banaras and trained some priestly musicians like Mithailallji and Bajpayeji. Banaras thus became a prominent centre of Classical Music.

Bahadur Hussain and Amir Khan who possessed some special skill in the use of *Alapa, Dhrupada, Dhamara* and in Instrumental Music, were invited with great respect and promise of princely allowances by Nawab Kalwe Ali Khan of Rampur. Bahadur Hussain was nephew of Pyar Khan Seni, the celebrated Sur-Sringar player, while Amir Khan was the son of Omrao Khan Seni, the renowned Veenkar. Bahadur Hussain concentrated on the instrumental music at Rampur and had a charming style of play. Some Musicologists say that his fingers were made of diamonds. He introduced many new Alankaras in the instrumental music and variations of Jhala or Jhankar which are unequalled even up to now by any Instrumentalist of India playing Sitar or Sarod. On the other hand Amir Khan Veenkar had a very melodious voice and, though originally an instrumentalist, his concentration was on Vocal Music. The Rampur *Gharana* of music was founded by these two musicians. Rampur subsequently, during the time of Haider Ali Khan, had a galaxy of musicians. Haider Ali Khan himself was a musician in the Vocal & Instrumental Music. During his time all other musicians in Rampur *Gharana*, the disciples of Bahadur Hussain and Amir Khan, although they belonged to other schools, adopted the style of their masters and thus became identified with Rampur *Gharana*.

All the musicians who became initiated in Rampur *Gharana* adopted the Raga system and the ways of execution of Tansen *Gharana*. So the Rampur *Gharana* may be said to be a special formation of the original Tansen *Gharana*.

CHAPTER II

TANSEN'S LIFE SKETCH

In musical genius and perfection Tansen's name is at the top. For centuries he has been known as *Swar Samrat* (king of melody). He has remained a luminary among the musicians of India of all times. In view of this it is unfortunate that not much is known about his early life.

About the place and year of birth of Tansen, there are many controversies. Banaras, Patna, Delhi and Gwalior are the places where Tansen is supposed to have been born.

His birth place according to one view is supposed to be Behat which is seven Kms. from Gwalior, as revealed by some of the Persian works of Akbar's time.[1] Abul Fazal has given the names of all musicians in the Court of Akbar and has mentioned in it that Tansen hailed from Gwalior. When he was very ill, Tansen expressed his desire before Akbar, to be sent to Gwalior. At that time Akbar did not agree to it keeping in view his health, but when he passed away, Akbar sent his body to Gwalior for last rites as per his wish.[2] This establishes that Tansen hailed from Gwalior. He further says that he was born in Brahmin family. From a work of that time, "252 Vaishavo Ke Varta" we have:-

सौ तानसेन बड़ी जाति वाले हते[3]

It shows Tansen was born in a Brahmin family. Tansen's Dhrupadas also give us the proof for this such as:-

---

1. "Akbar Darbar's Hindi Poets", Thesis published by Lucknow University.
2. Abul Fazal, "Ain-I-Akbari", p. 681.
3. Tansen Samaroh Gwalior, p. 23.

जै जै कर पूजौ धौलागढ़ की रानी ने
बीरबली वंश ब्रह्मण कुल तारन तानसेन वारदानी से [1]

His father's name was Makrand Pandey who was also known as Mukund Pandey, Mukund Misra or Mukund Ram.[2] The latter names seem to have been given to Makrand Pandey by the villagers of Behat as a mark of respect.

The problem of year of his birth is very complex. Different contradictory view points have been presented suggesting this or that year of his birth ranging between 1492 to 1531, a span of nearly four decades. Each view point is supported by references from books written in mediaeval period of Indian History.

Bhatkhande Ji has supported 1532, as the year of his birth.[3] This view is upheld in a booklet published on the Tansen-Samaroh and is also supported by a Research Thesis done in Lucknow University.

Brahaspati Ji has tried to prove that Tansen was born some where round 1492-1493. According to him Tansen joined Akbar's Court in 1562 A.D., when he was thinking to retire. His assumption is that a man should not like to retire in the prime of his life. It can be presumed that Tansen was contemplating to go into retirement in 1562, in advanced age.

Other reason given by Brahaspati Ji is that Lal Khan, son-in-law of Bilas Khan, the youngest son of Tansen, died in the third year of Jehangir's reign i.e. 1608[4], as per Fakirullah Khan, Lal Khan was more than seventy years of age at the time of his death[5] His year of birth may have been , 1538 A.D. Taking Lal Khan at least 15th years in age at the time of his marriage i.e. in 1553

---

1. Chaturvedi, Narmdeshwar, 'Sangeet Kaviyon Ki Hindi Rachanayen', p. 102.
2. Tansen Samaroh Gwalior, 1889, M.P. Govt. Publication.
3. Bhatkhande, Vishnu Narayan — 'Sangit Padhati.'
4. Brahaspati Acharya — 'Sangit Chintamani', pp. 282 - 283.
5. Fakirullah — Man Singh Aur Man Kutuhal, translated by Sri Narayan Chaturvedi, p. 135.

A.D., and the grand daughter of Tansen at least 10 years, Tansen was grand father in the year 1543 A.D. In the year 1562 A.D. he went to Akbar's Court i.e. 19 years after the marriage of Lal Khan with his grand daughter. His desire to retire in 1562 points to his fairly good age, which with 1492 as the year of his birth, could be (1562 minus 1492), 70 years. This logically seems in tune with his intension to retire.

In "Tavarikhay Kulliyat" and "Muntakhbutvarikhay" written by Al Badayuni in Akbar's time it is mentioned that Tansen got his title "Tansen" from Vikramajeet (reign 1516-1523), the son of Raja Maan Singh Tomar of Gwalior[1]. Ibrahim Lodhi besieged Badala Gadha which was the fort of Raja Vikramajeet. The siege lasted for more than four years and in A.D. 1523 Raja Vikramajeet accepted defeat. In A.D. 1526 both Raja Vikramajeet and Ibrahim Lodhi were killed in the battle of Panipat against Babar. This establishes, that Tansen in 1523 must have been of such age which could reasonally be appropriate to earn and receive the title, and so may have been born by the close of fifteenth Century.

TANSEN spent his early childhood in Gwalior. Early during the childhood he was like a pampered child of Mohd. Gaus. Mittal[2] referring to "Do Sau Vaisnava Ki Varta", states that when Tansen was five years of age, he began to learn music from a Mleccha (a Muslim). The name of the teacher is not mentioned. It is believed that Mohammad Gaus gave him training for nine years and for further training he sent Tansen to Swami Haridasa[3]. There are, however, many musicologists who categorically state that Mohammad Gaus would never have been Tansen's spiritual Guru. There are records like the "284 VAISNAVAS" to prove that Tansen's spiritual Guru was Govind Swami, while his musical Guru was Swami Haridasa. From the following composition of Tansen it is clear that Swami Haridasa was his Guru:-

---

1. Tvarikhay Kulliyat and Mutakhbuttvarikhay.
2. Mittal SSTJAR, p. 14.
3. Chobey Dr. Susheel Kumar, 'Sangeet Ke Gharano Ke Charcha' pp. 31-37.

पाई विद्या में परम, पुनि पाई है और अलख पाई है
गुरू हरिदास चरन निस्तारो है
मौको जगत पिता ने, तोको जगत माता ने दोऊ अधिकारी है
शिव गान संगत विस्तारो है
तेरी तान राम बान मदनराय उडगन समा और गुणी भाजे ।
भाजो है तानसेन, माता जीव दान देउ, तोरे लख मौको उभारा है।[1]

One of the legends is that Tansen by the age of five years, could mimic sounds of any bird or beast. One day Swami Haridaṣa along with his pupils was going through the fields of Tansen while on a visit to Gwalior, when Tansen started roaring in lion's voice. All the pupils of Swami Ji got scared but Swami Ji could not believe the presence of lion at that place and located Tansen. Tansen produced sounds of different birds and animals in front of Swami Ji. Swami Ji noted the potential of Tansen as a singer and requested his father to send Tansen along with him for training in music. Swami Haridasa gave training to Tansen and within ten years he got established as a top singer.[2] This legend also establishes that Tansen was a very good singer by the age of 15-18 years.

Tansen in later years of his life learnt music from Govinda Swami.[3] Govinda Swami was the follower of *Vallabha Sampradaya* and lived in *Varindvana* . *Al-Badaoni* writes that Adil which was the popular name of Sultan Mohammad Adil, king of Bihar (Reign A.D. 1549-1556), was a great master of singing and dancing.[4] Mian Tansen used to own being his pupil. From this it seems that Sultan Mohammad Adil was probably his teacher of music. Goswami Pannalal[5] mentions that "Swami Haridasa, who lived in Vrindavana had eight pupils. They were Baiju, Gopala, Lala, Madana Rai, Ramdasa, Divakara Pandita, Soma Pandita, Tanna Misra and Raja Sauka Sainji."

1. 'Sangeet Samrat Tansen', p.16.
2. 'Sangit Visharad', p. 303.
3. Mittal, Sangita Samrata Tansena Jivani Aur Rachanayen, Sahitya Sansthan Mathura, 1960, p. 14.
4. Al-Badaoni, Muntakhabu-T-Tawarikh, Vol.I, p. 557.
5. Pannalala Goswami, 'Nada Vinoda Grantha', Vol. II, p. 44.

Tansen had his early education in Music at the school of music founded by Raja Man Singh Tomar at Gwalior.[1] The historian, Smith, in his book "Akbar, The Great Mughul" mentions that Tansen had most of his early education at Raja Man Singh Tomar's School.[2] Only after his final training from Swami Haridasa, Tansen's name and fame spread all over India, as the foremost among the Kalawants of the age, (Master of Arts). This fact came to the notice of Akbar and it was reported to him that Tansen contemplated going into retirement and that he was spending his days in attendance on Ram Chand, the Rajah of Pannah. Akbar at once ordered that Tansen should be enrolled among the Court Musicians. Jalal Khan Qurchi, who was a favourite servant of Akbar, was sent with a gracious order to the Rajah for the purpose of bringing Tansen. The Rajah received the royal message and recognised the sending of *Tansen* as an honour. He sent to Akbar suitable presents of elephants of fame and valuable jewels, and he also gave Tansen suitable instruments and made him the cheek mole of his gifts.[3] He reached the Darbar of Akbar in 1562. Many historians of that time have mentioned it as a day of great importance during the time of Akbar's rule. The Iqbalnama says Akbar gave Tansen at his first assembly a Krore of dams, equal to two lakhs of rupees or 6,000 Persian tomans.[4]

Tansen was called by names such as Tanna Misra,[5] Ramtanu Trilochana[6] and Tan Singh[7] . Anyway the name by which he will always be remembered and cherished is Mian Tansen.

The name Tansen has a lot of significance as it has some

---

1. Abdl Fazal, 'Ain-i-Akbari', Vol. II, pp. 279-80.
2. 'Tansen Sangeet Samaroh', M.P. Govt., Publication, p. 23.
3. 'Akbar-nama', Translated by H. Beveridge, Vol. II, pp 279-80.
4. Abdl Fazal, 'The Akbarname', Vol. II, English Trans. refers to Iqbalnama, p. 230, Note 4.
5. 'Sangit Visharad'.
6. Deva B. Chaitanya, 'Indian Music', Vol. I, p. 57.
7. Al-Badaoni, Muntakhabu-T-Twarikh, English Trans. by Ran King, p. 557.

association with his ability of singing. Ustad Mushtaq Ali Khan says that it is believed that *TANSEN* got this title because his *TANAS* were very effective and perfect. *TAN* means *TANAS* and *SEN* means the finer edge of the sword. *TANSEN'S* style of singing and faster tanas were so accurate and to the point that it would pierce through the mind of list ner like the sword. Therefore he must have got his title of *TANSEN*.[1] The word *TAN* has a wider scope of meaning according to practical tradition of Indian Music. The literary meaning of *TAN* means stretching. The root is the musical idiom woven in musical compositions, whether it is a *Dhrupada* or a *Khayal* , have been referred to as the TANS by Ustads and professional musicians belonging to traditional families of musicians.[2] *TANNA MISRA* , *Ram Tanu* or *TAN SINGH* had already *TAN* with the childhood names and came to be known as *TANSEN* because his rare combination of superb practical music and an excellent "Vageykar".[3]

It becomes necessary here to mention that *TANSEN* was known as "Mian Tansen" either because of his conversion to Islam, or because of respect shown to him by the courtiers of Akbar at that time. Most of the ragas invented and developed by *TANSEN* have "Mian" before the name such as *Mian Ki Malhar, Mian Ki Todi,, Mian Ki Sarang* etc.

A common belief is that *TANA* was converted to *Islam* either when Peer Mohammad Gous blessed him by sharing his betal nut-roll[4] or when he married Hussaini, Brahmin, a maid servant of Queen Mriganayani, the widow of king Man Singh of Gwalior.[5] But none of the authors of that time has mentioned anything about his conversion to Islam. Prabu Lala Garg in Sangeet Hathras has written a convincing article to prove that Tansen remained a Hindu throughout

---

1. Based on Interview with Ustad Mushtaq Ali Khan Sahib of Calcutta.
2. Based on Interview with Dr. (Mrs.) Sumati Mutatkar, Ex-Dean & Head of Department, Faculty of Music & Fine Arts, University of Delhi.
3. Interview with Ustad Mushtaq Ali Khan Sahib of Calcutta.
4. Chàturvedi Narmdeswar, 'Kawi Tansen Aur Unka Kavya' p. 12.
5. Deva B. Chaitanya, 'Indian Music', p. 51.

his life. Moreover Abul Fazal as well as Mulla Badayuni in "Tuzukay Jahangiri" and "Ikbalnama Jahangiri " have not mentioned anything about Tansen's becoming Muslim.

One legend is that Tansen was married to Emperor Akbar's daughter, Mehrunissa. It is said that Tansen had to come to Akbar's Court against his as well as Raja Ram Chander's wish and did not wish to sing in Akbar's Court. To induce him into singing Akbar's daughter sang a raga in a wrong way when she knew Tansen was present near by. Tansen could not tolerate it and at once took DILRUBA from the hands of Mehrunissa and started singing Rag Basant. Akbar was also standing near by and he could not resist praising Tansen. Subsequently Akbar gave one crore of rupees and his daughter in marriage to Tansen. Same type of story is said about Swami Haridasa whose song Akbar wanted to listen.[1] There is no such mention in any of that books of that time.

Since Tansen's two sons *Tan-Tarang* Khan and Bilas Khan had the Muslim names and Tansen's grave or Samadhi still exists adjacent to Hazarat Mohammad Gous's grave, it cannot be said convincingly that Tansen did not become Muslim, and was known as "Mian Tansen" only because Mian is used generally as a mark of respect by Muslims.

It is somewhat enigmatic that while Tansen has been described in glowing praises by Sahasarasa, Al-Badaoni and Abul-Fazal, has called him unsurpassed musician, at the other places, in the same works, he is being mentioned as Atai or an ordinary musician. Abul-Fazal writes that a musician like Tansen has not been on this earth within a thousand years. In this work we also find the evidence of Tansen being acclaimed by Emperor Akbar as the greatest musician of India after the age of Bharata.

Sahasarasa states that during singing he always used to take other singers as aides and he did so even when he was asked to sing solo. Al-Badaoni in his Muntakhabu-

---

1. Chaturvedi, Narmdeshwar, 'Kawi Tansen Aur Unka Kavya', p. 15.

I-Tawarikh tells that one day a musician by the name of Shaikh Banjhu, who had a melodious voice and was a sufi tendencies and who was a disciple of Shaikh Adhan of Jaunpur, was introduced to Akbar. Akbar ordered him as well as Tansen and other great musicians to sing. In this contest Akbar found Shaikh Banjhu to be the best and, therefore, he ordered a pond, which had been built by Hakim Ali in Lahore to be filled with copper coins. These amounted to as much as twenty crores. Shaikh Banjhu was ordered to take away all that money, but he expressed his inability to carry away so much money. Instead he asked Akbar to give him some gold which it was easier for him to carry. The emperor granted the musician his wish.

Akbar also sent Shaikh Banjhu, Tansen and other great musicians to Shaikh Mubarak, the father of Abul-Fazal, for judging as to who among them was best. Shaikh Mubarak was unimpressed with the singing of Mian Tansen and described it as no better than the howls of wild beasts.[1]

In an era of brilliant poets, composers, and singers like Soordas, Ramdas, Tulsidas, Meerabai, Naik Baiju, Gopal Lal and others, Tansen's name stands out in real brilliance. Sweet and rapturous was his melody that it induced intoxication in some and sobriety in others.[2] Tansen must have reigned supreme since his music melody and voice could raise a listener to an ecstasy.

There are many verses showing the high esteem in which *TANSEN* was held by his contemporaries. Surdas Wrote:-

विघना अस जिय जान के, शेषहि दिये न कान

घरा मेरु सुन डोलती तानसेन की तान ।।[3]

meaning that earth and mountains all swing to Tansen's music. Tansen returned the compliment in this song:-

---

1. Al-Badaoni, Muntakhbut-i-Tawarikh, Vol. II, p. 273.
2. Goswami O, 'The story of Indian Music', p. 124.
3. Chaturvedi Narmdeshwar, 'Kawi Tansen Aur Unka Kavya', p. 15.

किधों सूर को सर लग्यों किधों सूर की पीर ।

किधों सूर को पद गयो, तन मन घुनत शरीर ।।[1]

A beautifully worded song at that time written by Sreepathy ends with the lines.

"AKBAR SHAHE NARAN PATHI"

"TANSEN TANAN PATHI"

meaning Akbar is the lord of men, Tansen is the Lord of musical notes.

In the Court of Akbar, Abdul Rahim Khan Khana, a great poet, wrote :-

धरा मेरु सुन डोलते तानसेन की तान

Praising Tansen's art, Hindi poet Gang wrote :-

तान् हद्दू तानसेन

These quotations leave no doubt in the mind about his greatness. In another book "Veer Bhanudaya Kavyam" Tansen has been mentioned as the greatest musician of the past, present and future. All these praises people must not have written just to please Akbar. Emperor himself said :-

पिघला सो मजलिस गयी तानसेन सो राग ।

हंसिबो, रमिबो, बोलिबो गयो बीरबल साथ ।।[2]

at the time of TANSEN's death, which shows how much respect and regard even great Mughal King Akbar had got for Tansen.

Al-Badaoni himself has written that Raja Ramachand, in whose service TANSEN was before joining Akbar, gave TANSEN in one day a crore of gold pieces for his singing ability. This statement has been corroborated by the author of the *Virabhanudaya Kavyam*. The author of the Virabhanudayam says that "for every song and each tana and each Dhrupada, he (Raja Ramachand), gave a crore of rupees

1. *Ibid.*
2. Chaturvedi Narmdeshwar, "Kavi Tansen Aur Unka Kavya", p. 16.

to this musician, namely Tansen, who was the embodiment of the art of music. Though the later statement seems to be exaggerated to some extent, yet from all this it is clearly understood that Tansen was a great musician.[1]

It is highly enigmatic and intriguing, that from some accounts it is concluded that Tansen was not best among the musicians during Akbar's time. At the same time we find him the best among all the musicians of past, present and future up to date. However it is concluded that accounts against Tansen have been partial and musicians and historians of that time have been unfair and jealous towards Tansen.

Tansen himself has acclaimed that Swami Haridasa surpassed him in singing. Gupta[2] , citing the testimony of books like "Bhaktamala-Haribhakti-Prakasika", "Bhaktamala-Kalpadruma", narrates an incident which tells us about Swamiji's musicial prowess. Once Emperor Akbar was so charmed by the music of Tansen, his Court Musician, that he asked Tansen if there was any musician on earth who was even better than Tansen. Tansen replied that Swami Haridasa could certainly sing better. At this Akbar expressed his desire to listen once to Swami Haridasa in the Royal Court. Tansen explained to Akbar that Swamiji was devotee of Lord Krishna and sang only for Him and that if the Emperor really wished to listen to him, Akbar would have to go to his Ashram. Akbar went in disguise of a Sadhu as the humble instrument carrier of Tansen. They came to the hermitage of Swami Haridasa on the bank of Yamuna, and Tansen asked him to sing, but he refused. Then Tansen practised a little trick and himself sang a piece before his old master, making a slight mistake in doing so. The master at once called his attention to it and showed him how to sing it properly and went on with the wonderful burst of song, while the Emperor listened enraptured.[3] Akbar found the music of Swamiji absolutely transcendental and lost himself completely. When Akbar regained his bearing he asked Tansen as to why he (Tansen)

---

1. Prajanananda Swami, 'A Historical Study of Indian Music', p. 177.
2. Gupta U. 'Krsnabhakti Kalina Sahitya Mein Sangita, Lucknow Visvavidyalaya, 1959, p. 42.
3. Popley Herbert, 'The Music of India', p. 17.

would not sing such a divine music. Tansen answered, "It is because I sing to please the emperor but gurudeva sings to please his soul in obedience to the inner voice".[1] This incident also points to the fact that Tansen was a great singer.

Beveridge writes that the first time Tansen performed at the Royal Court of Akbar, the Emperor presented him with two lakhs of Rupees.[2] Comparing the prices of essential commodities at the time of Akbar and the present prices in Delhi, a rupee of Akbar's time is equal to Rs.500/- to Rs. 1000/- (Varying from item to item as at present).[3] This means Tansen got Rs. Ten to Twenty Crores in his first concert.

Abul-Fazal writes that Tansen died on 26th April, 1586. On his death, at the instance of Akbar, all the musicians joined the funeral procession, and accompanied the dead body upto the grave singing and playing musical instruments as though it were a marriage festivity.

During the modern age the best musicians who perform all over the world, can record and get royalties etc. cannot earn Rs. 20 crores in whole of their life spans points to the fact that, Tansen who got so much money was one of the greatest musicians of all times. Accounts of life during the period when he was in Court of Akbar and afterwards have not been written impartially and facts about his life have got buried in the obscurity of history.

As per one anecdote, other musicians in Akbar's Court were very jealous of Tansen. Since Emperor always preferred Tansen, all musicians tried to drive a wedge between the two but all their efforts failed. Finally they asked Akbar that they want to listen Rag Deepak from Tansen. Tansen did not agree first but had no other alternative but to agree to the wish of Akbar.[4]

It is said the Deepak Raga which was sung by Tansen in Akbar's Court scalded the singer badly. This is proved

1. Srivastava Indurama, 'Dhrupada', p. 132.
2. Abul-Fazal, 'The Akbarnama', Vol. II, pp. 279-80.
3. Ain-I-Akbari, Sharma Harivansh Roy, Vol. I, p. 79.
4. 'Vasant Sangit Visharad', p. 304.

by the fact that the Late Ustad Mohammad Ali Khan, the descendant of Tansen, when challenged in A.D. 1928, to play Deepak Raga performed it on a Rabab in the temple of Hanuman at Gaya, and the flames evoked by the Deepak Raga burnt a part of the musical instrument, which has been preserved in the temple and is still worshipped.[1]

CONTRIBUTION

Upto the age of Tansen the composers of classical songs in India put proper value to the poetic aspect of the songs. During the Pathan period *Amir-Khusroo* the renowned poet and musician, introduced some *Persian* elements of music in *Delhi Darbar.* He composed numerous songs in the Persian style such as *Qaul Kalwana Qawwali.* Amir Khusroo composed new ragas by combining Indian and Persian melodies. During this time the Dhrupada form structured on the lines of *Shastric Prabandha* had come into existence. The *Dhrupada Padhati* received high respect in the context of temple music, where it was entitled as *Vishnupad.* However, it did not hold a dominant position in the Muslim Courts.

After the fall of Pathan Empire Raja Maan Singh Tomar of Gwalior established a musical school with four great learned and creative musicians. Their names were Nayak Bakshoo, Bhannoo, Mahmood Lohang and Karna.[2] The Dhrupada form of music got a status superior to that of the Qawwali during this period. It is evident that Tansen became an exponent of Dhrupada style and by his high creativity and genius raised the status of Dhrupada as the highest expression of music.[3]

Tansen was an outstanding force in the music of India. Goswami Ji states "He found Indian Music an unchartered ocean of Ragas and Raginis, which in his time numbered

1. Goswami O, 'The story of Indian Music', p. 245.
2. Faqirullah — 'Raag Darpan', p. 39.
3. Roy Chaudhuri Birendra Kishore, 'Indian Music and Mian Tansen', p. 12.

nearly 4,000. He examined each of them, analysed them and found many of them either repetitions of the main melodies or mere spurious creations without any scientific basis. He discarded the bulk of them and retained only 400. It was he who perfected the Indo-Muslim synthetic style of singing which later on was accepted as among the best and came to be known as *Darbari* .[1] None but a master mind like that of Tansen could have brought about such a complete systematisation of such an intricate art.

Birendra Kishore Roy Chaudhuri states "Tansen composed about 1000 Dhrupadas some of which are even now remembered not only for the wonderful exposition of the ragas contained in them but also for their very high poetic value. In the Hindustani Music field, the Dhrupadas composed by Tansen have brought him to the level of Tulsi Dasa and Surdas of Bhakti field as poet".[2]

Tansen was peerless and his compositions like Bach's music have the poetical quality which is very often epic in its sweep and some are tender and exquisitely lyrical in character.

Tansen based all his musical creations on the Dhrupada *Padhati* while assimilating some beautiful forms of the Persian music.

The theories of Tansen accept the view of the *Sangita Ratnakara* that Brahma created the *Marga* style of music out of the contents of the *Sama-Veda* which used to call the learning of music as the *Nada-Vidya*, the embodiment of the eternal spirit. The God Mahadeva was the original teacher of this Vidya and Paravati and Saraswati received this divine knowledge from him. In the teachings of Tansen we find accounts of the *Puranic* personalities like *Ravana*, *Valmiki*, Lava-Kusha, Hanumana, Arjuna and others. Then there are references of Bharata, Matanga, Sharangadeva and Kallinatha.

---

1. Goswami O, 'The story of Indian Music', p. 108.
2. Roy Chaudhuri, Birendra Kishore, Personal communications.

According to Birendra Kishore Roy Chaudhuri "Tansen based his theories of music accordingly on the *Shiva Mata* and the *Hanuman Mata* in which the exposition of the characteristics of the six main Ragas namely (1) BHAIRAV (2) MALKOSH (3) HINDOL (4) SHREE (5) MEGH (6) DEEPAK and their Raginis and the *Raga Putras* were given. Tansen regarded God Siva as the creator and Hanuman as the propagators of *Ragas* and *Raginis*". He was very devoted to God and Godesses which is revealed by his composition:-

अब मैं राम राम कह टेरों

मेरे मन लागो उन्हीं सीतापति पद हेरो ।

चरन सरोज श्रवन मन मेरो घुज अंकुस सुख केरो ।

तानसेन प्रभु तुम हो नायक इन भक्तन पर फेरो ।

Tansen had valuable contributions in the development of the instrumental music.

Both Basat Khan and Wazir Khan in their musical manuscripts have re-arranged the relations between Ragas and Raginis which they ascribed to Tansen's theories, in a way satisfying both reason and science.

According to Birendra Kishore, Tansen also assimilated some of the basic principles of the music of the middle east through Pir Mohammad Gous of Gwalior. The Arabic inspiration of this time shines as the milky way in the firmament of Tansen's music. Tansen reshaped the entire of Dhrupada music by addition of new ornamentations in MEEND, GAMAKA, etc. which was lacking till that time. His Dhrupada and Songs had special charms and emotional appeal.

In Ain-I-Akbari, Abul-Fazal says that Tansen made many improvements in Hindustani Music - For instance, he made a deep study of the four Mats of Dhrupad singing. These four Mats of raga-ragini system displayed great confusion regarding Raga and Raginis before the reign of Emperor Akbar. Birendra Kishore Roy Chaudhuri states, Tansen made a minute examination of the so called 1600 ragas and 360 Talas, studied the distinctive features of each raga and basic Talas. None but a master mind like that of Tansen could have brought about such a complete systematization of such an intricate art. The significant symbolism, beauty and subtlety of each raga and Tala is certain, popular and progressive.

Tansen created many new ragas which, uptill now are regarded as the formost Ragas of Northern India, some of these are note worthy such as :-

Darbari Kanhara, Darbari Todi, Mian Ki Malhar, Mian Ki Sarang, Mian Ki Todi, etc. Tansen had written three books:-

Sangit Sara, Raag Mala, Sri Ganeshastotra. We find also many outstanding Dhrupadas composed by him in praise of the Kings and Emperors.

While accepting the greatness of Tansen, it is still difficult to verify these statements like, "Tansen made minute examination of the so called 1600 Ragas and 360 Talas", in the absence of authentic documentary evidence.

A manuscript on music written by Tansen and based on Sangeet Ratnakar deserves mention. I got it when trying to find facts about Tansen.

Late Gopal Singh Ji a Pakhawaj player of Gwalior *Gharana* kindly allowed me to go through the manuscript and *Photostat* it for my use. A *photostat* copy is attached herewith. A brief Summary of its contents are given here.

The manuscript on music is based on Sangeet Ratnakar. To start with, Tansen defines the three branches of music, Vocal, Instrumental and Dance. He gives names of Ragas and says that music has originated from Brahma and believes that music gives the best and the highest pleasure of life. He adds that pursuit of music gives conforting experiences easily and leads even to liberation. He emphasises the gains from music flow with the blessings of Guru. He adds that it causes feelings of ecstasy and steers the sufferer to safety through storms in life.

He makes mention of the vibrations in views by seven Swaras and the laya and the harmony they are capable to forge.

He describes the tones and tunes of different types of music.

He enumerates the tones their traits and different Murchana's used in Ragas. Further he gives a list of main Ragas and Raginis, and their description such as, Bhairav, *Malkuans* , Hindol, Shree and Deepak.

He lays down the preferences in which the Ragas and Raginis be used. Further he prescribes different times for singing different Ragas. Next he gives details of different talas and how to use them.

Finally he gives a detailed list of musical instruments then in use, such as :- Been, Rabab, Swar Mandal, Tanbur, Dolak, Kartal etc.

The study of the manuscript is interesting and helpful to students of music.

॥श्री गणेशाय नमः॥ अथ संगीत रत्नाकर मतानुसारेण तानसेन कृत संगीत सार॥ सू
॥र मुनी को प्रणाम कर सुगम कियो संगीत॥ तानसेन सेरे सहित हित जाने गायन गीत॥
॥ गीत वाद्य अरु नित्त को कहो नाम संगीत॥ तानसेन उर धारि के मानो गायन चीत॥ द्
॥ प्रकार संगीत है मारग देशी जान॥ मारग ब्रह्मादिक के कहो देशी देश समान॥ अथ नाद लक्षण
॥ दो प्रकार को नाद है रा रवि सूर मुनि जान॥ तानसेन सो कहत है बहु विधि निहि बखान॥
॥ एक नाद जो मुक्ति दे दुजो रंजक जान॥ तानसेन रमणीय अति जानो ग्रंथ समान॥
॥ अनहद बाजत आपही आहत दिजो बजाय॥ तानसेन संगीत मत इन को यही सु
॥भाय॥ नाद अनाहद को सदा सुर मुनि करे जो ध्यान॥ गुरु प्रसाद सो मुक्ति दे यह जो नो परमान॥

34

सं० र
९

॥पवन अग्नि संयोगते प्रगट अनाहद नाम॥ तानसेन संगीत सब करत हे ताहि बखा
॥न॥ गीत बाद्य और निरत्यिको कह्यो जो आतम देह नो॥ तानसेन संगीत मत जामे उपज
॥त स्वाद॥ नाद उदधि को पार को केती करी उपाय॥ सिंधु तरन को सरस्वती तुंबा डर
॥हि कगाय॥ इडा पिंगला सु सुखमणा तीनो नारी नाम॥ तानसेन संगीत मत जानो
॥आबे काम॥ इडा वाम कहि पिंगला दक्षिण मनमे जान॥ सु हृदय रहत है सुषम
॥नाब्रह्म ग्रंथ जो मान॥ सप्त स्वर दोहा॥ खरज रिखभ गांधार अरु मध्यम पंचम जान॥
॥धैवत और निखाद है तानसेन परमान॥ औ उब कहिये पांच स्वर रवाउ नषट्
॥स्वर होय॥ तानसेन कहे सात स्वर संपूरन मिल होय॥ अथ हितीय भेद॥ दोहा॥

॥सप्त स्वरन को वेवरो सारिगमपधनी नाम॥द्वितीयभेद यातेकहत सुरवरति

॥नकोनाम॥अथजातसाधारण॥दोहा॥वादी विवादी संवादि कह्यो अनुवादी

॥पुन जान॥तानसेन संगीतमत चार विधीमन मान॥वादी अनुबादी कही वादी

य ॥शत्रु होवे॥अनुवादी जो मित्र है जानि लेव नर सोय॥संवादी राजा कहे विवादी प्र

॥धाने॥तानसेन संगीतमत कह्यो ग्रंथ परमान॥अरछाही आदि दै कह्यो अवरो

॥ही आरोहि॥संचारीमत तानसेन इनको कह्यो गिरोहि॥आरोही सुरचढत ही

॥उतर अवरोही होय॥तानसेन संगीतमत जानो गायन कोय॥आरोही अव

॥रोही लछन॥आरोही सारिगमपधनी रोही नीधपमगरि स होत॥आरोही

सं० रा०
२

॥ अब सोहि कहि तान सेन ऊधोत ॥ अथ ग्राम लक्षणं ॥ खर्ज को कहते ग्राम जो प्रगट भये
॥ हे तीन ॥ द्वै स्वर राख्यो अवनि पर एक खर राख्यो बीन ॥ गंधार नो ताको कहे सुरमुनि म
॥ राख्यो नाहि ॥ खर्ज ग्राम मध्यम कह्यो तान सेन हे याहि ॥ अथ स्वर उच्चार स्थान माह ॥ सेल ॥
॥ जानो खर्ज मयूर ते चात्रिक ऋखभ हि मान ॥ तान सेन संगीत मत कह्यो जियमें जान ॥
॥ अजा ते गंधार हो तहे काग ते मध्यम होत ॥ तान सेन संगीत मत कह्यो ग्रंथ विलोक ॥
॥ पिक ते पंचम होत हे धैवत दादुर भाख ॥ तान सेन संगीत मत कह्यो जियमें राख ॥
॥ गज ते कह्यो निखाद स्वर अंकुश लागे होय ॥ तान सेन संगीत मत जानो बुद्धि विलोय ॥
॥ अथ द्वितीय भेद लक्षणं ॥ उच्चार स्थानं ॥ खर्ज गंधार ज्यो सुर ताको कंठ स्थान ॥

श्री
२

॥ ॥ होमत व्याकरन तेत न सेन स्रुभ मान ॥ धैवत निरवान ॥ ...नन ते उरनम
॥ ध्यम जान ॥ पं॰ न॰ म ओ छ कहत है मत व्याकरन को मान ॥ सिरवभसी ते से आमियेक

॥ रकोद खो खान ॥ ... न सेन ओ कहत है सो मानो पर मान ॥ अथ ... नी दोहा ॥ रव

॥ जो पंचम मध्यम बिप्र बरन है सोई ॥ तान सेन बरनन करे बोलत सारद मुनि कोई ॥

॥ रुखवै धैवत छत्रि कह्यो तान सेन सो भाति ॥ कह्यो निसषभ नि षाद गांधार जव वैश्य
॥ कुलन मे जाति ॥ अथ गायन दोष लछनं ॥ रुछ निरस ककंश ... अस्थाई तो भ्रष्ट ॥
॥ गिरे अस्थान स्वर हीन अगुन कहाय तभ्रष्ट ॥ सो दिष्ट उदिष्ट अर सीतकार मत होय ॥

॥ संक्रम कंपित कराल जो औगुन गायन होय ॥ केपित्त का कवे नील सुर ऊर्ध्व

॥ चित्रकाव्ये ॥ सु खप्रमार और दसन रावि तानसेन यह के रव॥ दोहा॥ तानहीन
॥ रसहीन तानहीन स्वर काग॥ वदन भीर बंकोकि ए और समै को त्याग॥ और स
॥ दोरवविचार के ज्याको करो त्याग॥ तानसेन चतुर नर ताको है बड भाग॥ अथ
॥ गायन ॥ श्रद्धा और अभिलाष पुन सुमति कृपा सज्ञान॥ दयामें जोपरम
॥ सुख तानसेन उर ज्ञान॥ क्षमा चाली और सत्य सु रवबुधि द्रव्य विवेक॥ निश्चय
॥ भक्ति संयोग पुनि परचे भोग अनेक॥ सुधि बुधि औ तारसिक सुनन विचार
॥ सहीत॥ मन प्रसन्न आनंद जुत तानसेन सब मीत॥ गायन प्रकार तीन तें उत
॥ प्रमध्यम ज्ञान॥ तानसेन सं... ज्ञान कुं चतुर सुजान॥ रता सब विध स्तन है
॥ अ

॥मध्यम कहु कहीन ॥कनिष्ट सब तें हीन है तानसेन कहे बीन ॥ अथ श्रुति वर्णन॥
॥तिव्रा अरु कुमोद्वति मंदा जो है विचारि ॥ छंदोवती कहि खर्ज सुर तानसेन श्रुति चारि॥
॥दयावंती अरु रंजनी रतिका श्रुति है तीन ॥ रिखभ श्रुति जो होत है तानसेन परबीन॥
॥रुद्री क्रोधा श्रुति द्वै है श्रुति गंधार की होय ॥ तानसेन संगीत मत जानो गायन कोय॥ मध्य
॥म की श्रुति वज्रिका अरु प्रसारनि मानि ॥ प्रीति मार्जनी चारि श्रुत मध्यम की यह जानि॥
॥छिति रक्ता संदीपनी अरु आलापनि जान ॥ पंचम की श्रुति चारि है यह संगीत प्रमान॥
॥कहि मंदती रोहिनी रंभा श्रुति है तीन ॥ ये तो धैवत की कही सुर सुनि राखो बीन॥ द्वै श्रुति उ
॥ग्रा शोभनी कह्यो निखाद सो जान ॥ तानसेन संगीत मत श्रुति को यह परमान॥

पo २o
८

॥ अथ श्रुति लक्षनं ॥ करत उचार जो होत हे सुक्षम के अनुमान ॥ तान सेन संगी
॥ त मत श्रुति को यह परमान ॥ अथ मूर्छना वर्णनं ॥ मूर्छना तहा बसे हे जहां श्रुति को
॥ विश्राम ॥ तीन तीन स्वर प्रती रहे और बरनो तिन नाम ॥ आमोदनी प्रमोदनी विनोद
॥ नी और प्रमोदनी नाम ॥ खर्ज मूर्छना तान सेन उपजत स्वर विश्राम ॥ दीपी रक्ता प्राहि
॥ यत्र तीय संगवि चार ॥ यह मूर्छना रिखभ की तान सेन उर धार ॥ आरामिनी और का
॥ काभि विश्रामनि कोहे रख ॥ तान सेन मध्यम रहे ताको तुम भरोखे रख ॥ कोमनि रमैच्छाज
॥ मत्छायेपंचम स्वर मे ठान ॥ कहत मते संगीत मे सुनहु चतुर सुजान ॥ विस्तारिनी विता
॥ रिनी आधारनी पुन होय ॥ धैवत स्वर की मूर्छना बुधि मन मे जोय ॥ लज्जा संको

श्रीः
८
दि

॥ चौकहौ कपिलाकहौ बखान॥ सुनि खादल गहोत है कहत बडे परमान॥ अथ रागाध्याय॥
॥ प्रथम भैरव पुन मालकोश हि हिंडोल दीपक श्रीराग॥ मेघ राग पुनि तानसेन यह पुरु
॥ षब्ड भाग॥ भैरव की भार्या॥ मधुमाध पुन भैरवी बंगाली अभिराम॥ बरारी अरु सैंध
॥ वी भैरव की यह बाम॥ मालकंस भार्या॥ टोडी और खंबावती गौडी गुनकली नाम॥
॥ ककुभ सहित यह तानसेन मालकोश की बाम॥ हिंडोल भार्या॥ वेलावली और राम
॥ कली पटमंजरी देशाख॥ तानसेन यह लकित पुनि हिंडोल संग भाख॥ दीपक भार्या॥
॥ नटमल्हारी कानरा केदारा अभिराम॥ देशी पहाडी तानसेन दीपक की यह बाम॥॥
॥ श्री राग भार्या॥ वसंत मालवी मालश्री धनाश्री पुन संग॥ आसावरी तानसेन श्री राग ल्हे हरंग॥

॥अथमेघभार्या॥मल्हारदेशकारीभूपालीपुनजान॥बडहंसगुर्जरटंककहेमेघरागसं
॥गमान॥अथइंद्रप्रस्थमतरागरागिणी॥अथषट्‌रागनाम॥पहिलेभैरवरा॥
॥हे दुजेकौशिकजान॥त्रतीयहिंदोलबखानियेचौथेदीपकमान॥पंचमश्रीरागकहेछठेमे
॥घप्रमान॥पांचपांचभार्याकही अष्टपुत्रप्रतिजान॥भैरवीरामकलीपुनदोउगुर्जरीना
॥भैरवरागकीरागिणीमतसंगीतहिसारि॥रवंभावतीबागेश्वरीककुभपरजमनमान॥
॥कह्यो मतसंगीततेऔरशोभनीजान॥प्रथमवसंतीपंचमीदेवगांधारीविभासकाहि॥
॥ललितदेशाखीसंगलेलिंहिंदोलकीनारि॥धनाश्रीमुलतानीनटीजयतश्रीपुनआ
॥नं॥भीमपलासी रागिणीदीपकसंगबखान॥मालवीत्रिवणीगौरिकापूरवीटंकी

॥ दान॥ श्रीरागकी रागिणी संगीतमतमान॥ सोरट मल्लारी कहिये सारंग बडहंस मान॥
॥ बडहंस सोम धुमाधनी मेघ योषिता जान॥ नट नारायण मेघ में गाइये भैरव प्रथम स्वराग॥
८ ॥दिन भैरवी रामकली पटगुनकली अनुराग॥ देशकार विभास पुन भटि
॥यारी बरवार॥ बसंत बहार और पंचम माहि॥ जो डोल हिंडोल कारा॥ बेकायवली अ
र ॥डाणा कान्हरा कंभ॥ देवगिरि ललिता भूपाली सुहाग हरिगाज॥ गुलाब धुरियाखाँ॥
॥खटकाश भोरा खबुन रामकली प्रभा रव॥ रामनाथ सुघरयी सुही भूपाली देवगिरि
॥गंधार लोभाष॥ दिन पहर रात दिन पट ढोली दोडी गुर्जरी गान॥ देशी आसाव
॥रिजोनपुरी बराडी टोडी जान॥ सारंग गुर्जरी बृंदावनी बडहंसी सावंत॥ राम॥

॥लंके दहन वृूमल्हू कुर दोपहरे मे वंत॥मेघमल्हारी गोड पुन गौड गिरी जल धार॥
॥नट मल्हारी सूर पुनि रामदासी मल्हार॥सुहुतानी और धना श्रीभीमपलासी
॥जान॥बरवा धानी अहिरिको तृतीय प्रहर करगान॥जैगल्हा मंगल पीलू पुनै ॥श्र
॥सिंधु तैं केगपर दीप॥दीपक दीपकी काफी पुनः चौथे प्रहर प्रकीप॥जेतश्री ॥८
॥ऋषी मालश्रीमालश्री गोराह॥गोड सारंग मारवा पुरबी औ पूरवाह॥त्रिवणी
गो ॥श्री रीबहुरी चेतीटंकी मान॥चौथेप्रहरदिन अंतमे श्रीटंक करगान॥प्रथम
गा ॥जामर जनी समेकल्याण सुधवैन॥हेमक्षेम एमन पुन श्याम हे मो रही जान॥
॥जैत भूपाली पुरीयाको केदकरब गान॥प्रहर रजनी जाने गुनी छायानाट्टं वखान॥

॥ दूहण पत रजनि शिके समे नायकी वक्त प्रमान ॥ अष्टादश लेका न्हराकों शीकका न्हर
॥ जान ॥ आडाना सहना सोभना सोहन सोहनी मान ॥ केदारा मल्लोहा पुननाटके
॥ दार बखान ॥ बिहाग बिहागरा बिहारि पुन विहाग पुन विनोद ॥ भरन अरन संकी
॥ र्णो अरु शंकरा अमोद ॥ सोरट दे श सो राष्ट्र कासिं दुरा साभेरि ॥ पाल्नर्वं भावती ख़ावा
॥ वती कालिंगरा आभेरि ॥ मालकौ श और को श की कुस म का सम्पूर्ण दी ॥ कालिंगा
॥ कलिंगा कौ कावरी अरुणोदय में बाटि ॥ सो एक सत त्रि और आ बसो राग रागि
॥ णी जान ॥ देश देश के भेद मे भिंन्न भिन्न तेनाम ॥ मारग ग्रन्थादिक कहे देशी दिश है
॥ धाम ॥ अनुद्रुत ० द्रुत ० वराम ० पुनि लघु ० लघुवराम ० गुरु ३ बखान ॥ तीन सो सा

सं० २०

॥७ प्रसिध्धेरे आदि तालादि प्रमाण॥ एक ताल धमार पुनि रूपक और तितार॥ श्री फ्र

॥ क भूपजार औ चौताल अठताल॥ के दस वार रुद्र ब्रह्म रिकापंच मुखाष इक तार॥

॥ समा अष्टाल क्ष्मी पुन ब्रह्म ताल दश तार॥ अथ मार्ग ताल नामानि॥ पंच ता

॥ ल मारग कहे शिव मुख ते प्रगट होय॥ तान सेन संगीत मत कहत सब हि गिनाय॥

॥ पंच पुरुष हल्लीसक कहत हे पुन चाचपुट ही जान॥ तान सेन संगीत मत कहो ग्रन्थ

॥ प्रमान॥ षट्पितापुत्रक कहे उदघट्ट संपक धार॥ तान सेन संगीत मत मारग ता

॥ ल विचार॥ ताल नामानि॥ आदिताल द्वितालक पुन त्रितीय चतुर्थ होय॥ पंचम च

॥ निःशंक सिंह विक्रम तान सेन कहे सोय॥ रति लील सिंहनन्द की कहे कंदर्प

॥सिंहवीरविक्राम॥श्रीरंग और चंचरी तानसेन सुरधाम॥राजताल और वर्णता
॥लसिंहविलत गजझान॥दर्पण मिश्रवर्ण हतानसेन परमान॥जयवनमालीताल
॥हे हंसनादसिंहनाद॥कुडुक तुरंगलीलतानसेन सरभलीलहे स्वाद॥सिंहनंद
॥ननंदनत्रिभंगा पुनरंगाभरणवा मंठ॥मुद्रित मठविधो मंठतानसेन करकंठ॥क्रो
॥किलप्रियनिशाकर राजविद्याधर जान॥तानसेन जयमंगलाविजयानंद बखान॥
॥मल्लिकौं मोदकी डाजयमकरंकी रतिनाम॥श्रीकीर्तिप्रतितालपुनतानसेन अ
॥भिराम॥बिजयबिदुरसमनंदनब ~~मकरंद~~ मठीकावा मंठ॥दीपकछेकी विषमसु
॥नतानसेन श्रीकंठ॥अभिनंदन अनंगपुनि नांदिमल्लिताल॥तानसेन पूरण कही

सं० र०
८

॥पुनखंडकें काल॥विषम लघु शेखर कहे चतु भा धीकें को लु॥काहुक एक कुसु
॥द पुन तानसेन चतु साल॥बाकुंद और शेखली रायबंक अभंग॥तानसेन बसंतपुन
॥अति शेखर त्रिभंग॥प्रताप शेखर भूपताल है गज झंपा पुन होय॥चतु र्दु विराति
॥तानसेन मंद ताल हे सोय॥प्रति मठ वा प्रति मठ पारवती लो चन होय॥लीलाक
॥रण अति ललित तानसेन हे सोय॥राजनारायण गारुडा लक्ष्मी दसवरमा
॥न॥लद्दित्ती प्रयायत तानसेन व धन जनक प्रमान॥उत्त सवविलोकित
॥वर्णयति तानसेन सिंह जान॥करणा सारस चंडहे चंद्रकला जयजोय॥
॥स्कंध द्रुताली हृदु धुन तानसेन यह होय॥सुकुंद कुबिद कन्द ध्वनि गौरी

श्री
८

॥ ... ॥ ... तानसेन भयताकु पुनहोत ॥ तानकीकंठ

७१ भरेही औरराजमामेंहु ॥ तानसेननिसंक पुनरत्ताकरतहमेंठ॥

॥ अथमतीतानरकृततैहि चित्रके हुक रहु उवान ॥ संन्निपात भई तो

॥ ... पुत्र तानसेन परमान ॥ चतुरंग ... अर्जुन बकुर अकुन संत्रि

॥ म आसन्नि ॥ ... कल्याण पुनि तानसेन वासन्त ॥

॥ ... धातवापे-च धात चंद्रताकु गणमें ठ॥ एक ताको कहि-चतुर

॥ ... धतानसेन करमंन ॥ राम-चंद्रप्रसिंह हे चिपुका पुन मनमान॥

॥ ... तानसेनसंगीतमतक ... जियमेंजान ॥ पतिसें चयपठताकी

॥ कापृथ्वीकुं उठकीहोय ॥ तानसेन ... मत मतम भएथ्वीकुं उठकीपुनहोय ॥॥

॥ ... ॥ ... कु उठकीकतेपाताकुं उठकीकार ॥ तान

सेनसंगीतकतेंजियमेंदेवविचार ॥ विष्णु ... बनतारिकानिकल ...

॥ ... ॥ तानसेन उठव पुनि कनकमेंकचलताय ॥ कनकमेंतवा...

८६ ॥ को पुन चक्रमें ... ताये ॥ शरबसंयोग चतुर स्वहे तानसेनरसाठ ॥ वि श्री ९

... धरमठ बामठ चतुरमठ श्रीविष्णु ॥ मन्मथ हंस सरस्तनु पवि ष्णुमं ...

॥ होय ॥ द्रुतपर्ण कहीतानसेनरति तुष्ठ पुनहोय महाविचित्र ...

॥ ... बैरतन ॥ अभंगशेखर हंस नाद पुनि तानसेन धरमेन ॥ मेघे

॥कमला कुमुद कहि कि ल्ह कंठ मसिस्थ ॥मंठ ताल्हा पनि मंठ पुन तानसे
॥न प्रथरिस्थ ॥विजयमंठ सां ल्हंग पुनि सरस मंठ ॥ पडि मंठ ॥ कील्हक मंठर
॥विमंठ कहि तानसे नहरि मंठ ॥जनक मंठ यज मंठ कहै प्रिय मंठ श्री मंठवि
॥ राजयगनो ॥ रंगवर्णगी वीण कल्याण कमल्ह विशाल्हव छ्कु भमनमानो ॥
॥ कल्हापविचित्र मुद्रित गंभीर श्री रंगभूभिन्न कविवर्णही जानो ॥ संकी
॥र्णकलिंग विल्होकी पराजय ये सब मंठ के नाम बखानो ॥ रुद्र ताल्ह कुरणाय त्री
॥क छपताल्ह बखान ॥ तानसेन कहे सरस्वती कंठाभरण प्रमाण ॥ नारद शार
॥द तुंबर किन्नर ताल्ह विचार ॥ तानसेन यह कहत तरन को कोहु न पावे पार ॥ इती

सं० र०

१

॥ ताळनामानि ॥ अथ कळावंत द्वादशताळमाह ॥ एकताळ द्विताळ तताळ चतु
॥ र्थ होय ॥ त्रेवट अठताळी कहे सुर्फाकताळ होय ॥ पट्ताळी धमारिका सपयतिथी
॥ माळ ॥ गन ॥ कवि शब्द शोन वरन करे जान कु चतुर सुजान ॥ भाषा प्रसिध्द दे
॥ श वर्तमान माह ॥ प्रथम चौताळ प्रसिध्द हे आड चौताळ बखान ॥ रू
॥ पक बहुरी जानी मे वडे ताळ मन मान ॥ झंपताळ सुर्फाक ता त्रेवट ताळ समे
॥ त ॥ शब्द सेन बर्नन करे राग ताळ के हेत ॥ जळद तिताळा धीमा कहे पट जत ताळ
॥ बखान ॥ होळी आड एक ताळ पुन द्वादश ताळ प्रमान ॥ इति कळावंत द्वादश ताळ
॥ नामानि ॥ इती श्री राग सागरो द्भव ताळ नामानि संपूर्णानि ॥ अथ प्रबंधाध्याय प्र
कर्ण ॥

श्री
४

॥ताळराग कोमूळ है बाद्य ताळ को अंग॥ तानसेन वाद्य ताळ दो उन्नस्यत उब

॥ततरंग॥ अथ वाद्यभेद नामानि॥ तत्त को पहिले कहत है वित्तत दुसरी ठान॥

॥तीज घन चैथे शिुखर तानसेन परमान॥ तार ळगे सब साज के सो तत तही

॥नुममान॥ चरमम दो जाको मुरख वितत कहे बखान॥ कैसताळ के आदि दे

॥घन जीय जानहु मीत॥ तानसेन समीर रस बाजत शिखर सुनीत॥ तत

॥नामदोहा॥ बिनपीनाकर बाजे है सर मंडळी साढ रंगी॥ चार तांत ते बुरपुन तानसेन उपंगी॥

॥अमृत कुंडळी चंग ओर आबझ और अनेक॥ तानसेन संगीनमत जानो बुद्धि

॥विवेक॥ अथ वितत नामानि॥ मृदंग ढोळकी दुंदुभी दारा खंरी जान॥

सं॰ र॰
१६

॥ चंगल्डा डुर अनेक है तान सेन उरमान ॥ अथ घन नामानि ॥ कांसताळ ओ नसा
॥ झपुन कहे गुनी कटतार ॥ बाजत नी के तान सेन यह घन सम झि विचार ॥ अथ
॥ शिनवर नाम ॥ बेनु बासरी नाद है स्वरनाई कर मौल ॥ भुंगळ तुरही न्रसिंगा शिरव ना
॥ रहे और मुरचंग रसाळ ॥ अथ वाद्य नाम कवीत ॥ बीन आपीनाक ते रबाब सुरमंडळी ॥ श्री
॥ सारंगी दुतार ओर तंबूर उपंग अम्रत कुंडळी ॥ अब मृदंग ढोलकी दुंदुभि दारा ठपा शिख ११
॥ ..गजे है ॥ खंजरी कताळ और कठताळ झांझ झनक ओर बेनु बासरी सो नादगाज
॥ है ॥ सुरनाई कनोळ तुरही ॥ मुरचंग न्रसिंगा मिळ सब ब्रजमंडळ मे भाजति ॥ वाद्य भेद
॥ के नाम कहे सुन हो चतुर सुजान ॥ शिव को भाषित है सबे मत संगीत प्रमान ॥ ५२ ॥

GENEALOGICAL TREE CHART OF SENIA GHARANA

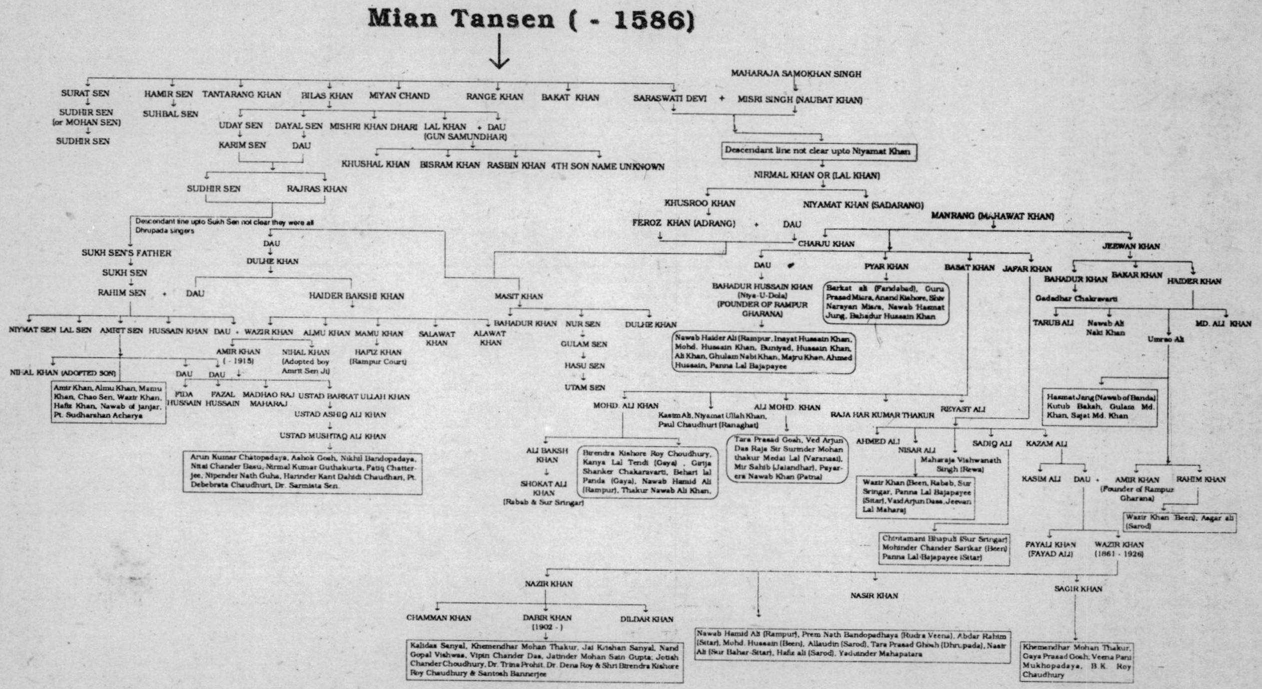

Note :

1. Names of Musicians of Tansen's progeny are in Capital Letters
2. Names of other disciples are in small letters

तानसेन कृत ध्रुपद "यमन कल्यान" चौताल [1]

तकत हूँ तिहारी आस, दास जनम–जनम के । हमारे दुख हरो साकी होज़े कौसर के ।।
तुमसो जू कौन और, जिस जाय कहूं दौर । हमको तो नहीं ठौर, बिन पायन पर के ।।
सब दुख निर्वारिन को, पाप पखारन को । तनमन वारन को, शवीर शवर के ।।
इतना प्रसाद मांगत मियां तानसेन । बांह गही मोरी अब मत करो दर-दर के ।।

स्थाई

								प			
						ध	प	मं	ग	रे	ग
						त	क	त	हूं	-	ति
						3				4	
प	ग	प	-	प	-	प	-	ध	प	मंप	प
हा	S	S	S	री		आ		स	दा		स
				2		0		3		4	
प	ध	ध	सां	नी	ध	प	धप	मं	ग	मं	ध
ज	न	म	ज	न	म	के	S	S	S	S	ह
X		0		2		0		3		4	
				रे							
प	—	प	रे	ग	मं	ग	रे	ऩी	रे	सा	-
मा	S	रे	S	दु	S	ख	S	ह	S	रो	
X		0		2		0		3		4	
			प	म				रे			
सा	प	धपु	मं	ग	मं	ग	रे	सा	रे	सा	ऩी
सा	की	S	S	S	S	S	S	हो	S	जे	S
X		0		2		0		3		4	
				सा							
ध़	ऩी	ग	रे	ऩी	सा						
कौ	S	स	र	के	S						
		0		2							

1. मारिफुन्नग़मात, दूसरा भाग, पृष्ठ 13-14.

अन्तरा

प	प	सां	ध	सां	सां	सां	-	सां	सां	-	सा
तु	म	सो	S	S	जू	कौ	S	न	औ	S	र
X		0		2		0		3		4	
		रें		·					रें		
सां	सां	ग	रे	गं	में	गं	-	रें	सां	रें	सां
जि	स	जा	-	य	क	हूं	S	S	दो	S	र
X		0		2		0		3		4	
							प				
सां	नी	नी	ध	प	घ	प	मं	ग	मं	ग	रे
ह	म	को	S	तो	न	हीं	S	ठौ	S	र	S
		0		2		0		3		4	
ग	मं	प	नि					प	नि		
रे	ग	मं	ध	रे	-	सां	नी	मं	ध	नी	ध
बि	न	पा	S	S	S	य	न	प	र		
X		0		2		0		3		4	
			प	मे							
प	-	घुपु	मं	ग	मं						
के	S	S	S	S	S						
X		0		2							

संचारी

	मैं										
ग	ग	प	-	प	प	प	प	प	मैं	ध	प
स	ब	S	S	दु	ख	नि	र	वा	S	र	न
X		0		2		0		3		4	

प	-	प	मैं	धं	सां	नी	ध	प	ध	प	धप
को	S	पा	S	प	प	खा	S	र	न	को	S
X		0		2		0		3		4	

प	मैं	ग	ग	रे	ग	मैं	ग	रे	नी़	रे	सा
S	S	त	न	S	म	न	वा	S	र	न	को
X		0		2		0		3		4	

						नि़				सा	
सा	-	ग	रे	सा	नी़	ध़	नी़	ग	रे	नी़	सा
श	S	बी	S	र	S	श	S	व	र	के	S
X		0		2		0		3		4	

आभोग

प	प	सां	-	ध	सां	सां	-	सां	रे	-	सां
ह	त	ना	S	S	S	प्र	S	सा	S	S	द
X		0		2		0		3		4	
		रें							सा		
सां	-	गं	रें	गं	में	गं	रें	सां	नी	रें	सां
मा	S	ग	त	मि	यां	ता	S	न	से	S	न
X		0		2		0		3		4	
		ध					प	में			
सां	नी	नी	ध	प	घ	प	म	ग	मे	ग	रे
बां	S	ह	S	ग	S	ही	S	मो	S	री	S
X		0		2		0		3		4	
ग	में	प	नि					प			
रे	ग	में	ध	रे	-	सां	नी	में	ध	नी	ध
अ	ब	म	त	S	S	क	रो	द	र	द	र
X		0		2		0		3		4	
			प	मे							
प	-	धप	में	ग	मे						
के	S	S	S	S	S						
		0		2							

तानसेन कृत ध्रुपद "भूपाली", चौताल[1]

बानी चारों के व्यौहार सुन लीजे हो, गुनीजन तब पावे ये विद्यासार ।
राजा गोवरहार फौजदार खण्डार दीवान डागुर बक्सी नवरहार ।।
अचल सुर पंचम, चल सुर रिषभ, मध्यत धैवत निषाद गंधार ।
सप्तक तीन ऐकीस मूर्छना, बाईस श्रुति उनंचास कूटतान तानसेन अधार ।।

स्थाई

सा	रे	सा	ध़	प़	ग	ग	रे	ग	रे	सा	-
बा	S	नी	S	चा	S	रों	S	के	S	व्यो	S
3		4		X		0		2		0	
सा	रे	सा	ध़	ग	रे	ग	सारे	ग	-	प	ध
हा	S	र	S	सु	न	ली	S	जे	S	हो	S
3		4		X		0		2		0	
प	ग	रे	ग	रे	सा	सा	ध़	प़	–	ग	रे
गु	नी	ज	न	त	व	पा	S	वे	S	ये	S
3		4		X		0		2		0	
ग	प	ध	–	प	ग	ग	रे	ग	सारे	ग	रे
वि	S	S	S	द्या	S	सा	S	S	S	S	र
3		4		X		0		2		0	

1. मारिफुन्नग़मात, दूसरा भाग, पृष्ठ 17–18.

अन्तरा

		सां									
ग	प	ध	सां	सां	-	सां	सां	-	सां	रें	सां
रा		जा	S	गो	S	व	र	S	हा	S	र
X		0		2		0		3		4	
		सां									
सां	ध	घ	सां	–	सां	सा	ध	सां	सां	–	सां
फौ	S	ज	दा	S	रे	खं	S	S	डा	S	र
X		0		2		0		3		4	
गं	रैं	गं	रैं	सां	सां	ध	सां	सां	सां	घ	प
दी	S	वा	S	न	डा	S	गु	र	व	क	सी
X		0		2		0		2		4	
ग	प	ध	सां	ध	प	ग	रे	ग	सरे	ग	रे
S	न	व	र	हा	S	S	S	S	S	S	र
X		0		2		0		3		4	

संचारी

ग	ग	ग	गर	ग	ग	प	रे	ग	रे	-	सा
अ	च	ल	सु	S	र	पं	S	S	च	S	म
X		0		2		0		3		4	
						ग					
सा	सा	ध़	सा	-	सा	रे	ग	-	रे	-	सा
च	ल	S	सु	S	र	रि	S	S	ख	S	ब
X		0		2		0		3		4	
सा	रे	सा	ग	-	ग	ग	प	ध	S	प	ग
म	ध्य	म	धै	S	व	त	नि	शा	S	द	S
X		0		2		0		3		4	
प	ध	सां	ध	सां	-	ध	-	प	ग	-	-
गं	S	S	S	S	S	धा	S	र	S	S	S
X		0		2		0		3		4	

आभोग

ग	प	ध	सां	-	सां	सां	सां	-	ध	सां	-
स	प्त	क	ती	S	न	ए	की	S	स	मू	S
X		0		2		0		3		4	
								सा			
सां	सां	ध	सां	रें	गं	रें	सां	ध	सां	घ	प
र्छ	ना	S	बा	S	ई	S	स	श्रु	S	ति	S
X		0		2		0		3		4	
ध	प	रे	ग	-	रे	ग	प	ध	सां	ध	सां
उ	नं	S	चा	S	स	कू	S	ट	ता	S	न
S		0		2		0		3		4	
सां	-	सां	ध	-	प	ग	रे	ग	सारे	ग	रे
ता	S	न	से	S	न	अ	घा	S	S	S	र
X		0		2		0		3		4	

In this Dhrupada of Tansen, there is the mention of the seven Chapters of Sangita Ratnakara of Sharangdeva.

नाद अगाध संपूर्ण सोध साध समझ सोच लाल विस्तार ओंकार ।।
सुर सवार सप्त सलिल सुर सुर सों संगत नाद विस्तार ।।
स्वर धाय राग ध्याये ताल ध्याय नृत्य ध्याय प्रकीर्ण
प्रबन्ध मृदंग ध्याय सप्त ध्याय विचार ।।
गुनी गंधर्व सुर नर मुनि पच हारे केऊ न पायो तानसेन अपरंपार ।।"[1]

The art of music is infinite yet complete. A learner should carefully understand its rules concerning rhythm and should always remember God. First he should master the seven notes because this is the backbone of music and after this he should study the *Saptadhyaya, Svaradhyaya, Ragadhyaya, Talaadhyaya, Nrthadhyaya Prakirnaadhyaya* (Chapter on miscellaneous topics), *Prabandhadyaya* Chapter on Compositions) and *Mrdangadhyaya* Chapter on Instruments). Many experts tried to master its intricacy but nobody could do so. Tansen says this art is limitless.

In this Dhrupada Composition which is in Raga Malkauns *(Choutal)* Mian Tansen addresses Baiju Bawra and wishes to know about the origin of the *Svara's* and use of Ascent and Descent in singing.

ऐजू खरज कहां ते, कहां ते रिखभ
कहां ते उपजौ गंधार, मध्यम कहां ते, पंचम कहां ते
उपज्यौ धैवत निखासा, आरोही कहां ते
अवरोही कहां ते, उपज्यौ कहां ते गीत सार
कहे मियां तानसेन, सुनो बैजू बावरे
को जाने जाकौ विस्तार ।। [2]

1. Chaturvedi, Narmadeshwar :- Sangeetaghya Kaviyoon Ki Hindi Rachnayein, p. 110.
2. Collection of late Gopal Singh Ji, Pakhawaj Player Gwalior Gharana.

In this Dhrupada Baiju Bawra names the parts of the body from which the *Svara's* originate in reply to the enquiry made by Tansen, and adds that God Mahadeva first made use of Alankar's.

बैजू :-

खरज नाभि तें, रिखभ हृदय तें
गरे से उपज्यौ गंधार, मध्यम मुख से
पंचम नासिका ते, धैवत निखार
ब्रह्माण्ड सार, कोमल कंठ से
तीव्र तालू से, जै सुर लेवे संभार के ।
कहे बैजू बाबरे सुनो मियां तानसेन
महादेव प्रथम कहयो अलंकार ।

CHAPTER III

SENIA GHARANA

DESCENDANTS OF TANSEN AND SENIA GHARANA

The *Senia Gharana* is one which has strictly followed the teachings of *Mian Tansen* through his descendants and disciples who adopted the unique style of singing of *Dhrupada* and playing instrumental music of Tansen tradition, having enriched, modified and invented new styles of singing and new instruments after TANSEN till today.

The descendants who have adhered to the style of *Tansen's* School of music are known as *Senia's* of *Senia Gharana* . Senia Gharana was formed by the disciples and descendants of Tansen's sons and daughters.

Genealogical tree charts are drawn to trace the line of Bilas Khan and Misri Singh down to the present day musicians. Unfortunately not much could be known about the descendants from the year 1667-1668 onwards when, it is believed, that Aurangzeb banned music in his court. During this period Faqirullah wrote Raga Darpana while the next book on music and musicians was written in 1855 by Hakim Karam Imam. These two have mentioned Saraswati Devi, daughter of Tansen, and her descendants. It is questionable whether Tansen had any daughter. Brahaspati Ji, has pointed out that Saraswati Devi and Misri Singh were a creation of certain musicians to prove their heritage so as to get adjusted in different courts as Court Musicians. In any case no old reference is available upto Niyamat Khan (Sadarang) among the descendants of Misri Singh.

The other point which is worth noting is that many authors in the twentieth Century have mentioned Rahim Sen as son of Masit Khan while as Sudarshan Acharya, in his book Sangeet Sudarshan, has mentioned that Rahim Sen was son of Sukh Sen, whose father and grand father were Dhrupada singers and descendants of Bilas Khan while as Masit Khan was descendant of Tansen's daughter.[1] If Rahim Sen *was* the son or grand son of Masit Khan or, for that matter, a descendant of Misri Singh, then Bilas Khan's line after Rajras Khan is not traceable. Considering the writings of authors, all musicians after Niyamat Khan Sadarang, who presently claim to be the descendants of Tansen's sons line, would have been the descendants of Misri Singh, if Rahim Sen were the son or grandson of Masit Khan.

It has also not been possible to trace the parentage and line of Nirmal Shah a great Veena player and a cousin brother of Pyar Khan, Basat Khan and Jafar Khan. Although Bimal Kant Roy Choudhuri[2] has shown Nirmal Shah as grandson of Bhupat Khan and Bhupat Khan as son of Niyamat Khan, but as per Hakim Karam Imam[3], Charju Khan and Jeevan Khan were the grandsons of Niyamat Khan and their sons, in turn, were Pyar Khan, Basat Khan, Jafar Khan, Bahadur Khan and Haider Khan.

Most of the musicians now attribute to this mix-up and confusion the reasons that Bilas Khan and Misri Singh were in close touch with each other after the death of Tansen till the Bilas Khan's line took to Veena also and Misri Singh's line took to Rabab also. Misri Singh also became a Mohammadan. The inter marriages among these two families and descendants having no particular surname and a gap of around 200 years between the authors, Faqirullah and Karam Imam, have resulted in much of the confusion.

---

1. Acharya Sudarshan, "Sangit Sudarshan", p. 18.
2. Roy Chaudhuri, Bimal Kant, 'Bhartiya Sangeet Kosh', p. 171.
3. Hakim Karam Imam, 'Mudunul Mausiqui, p. 32.

However from the references available, Genealogical tree charts have been drawn for Tansen and his descendants. The chart is attached at the end of this Chapter. Here, prominent descendant musicians in the line of Tansen are discussed.

Tansen had four sons. Abul-Fazal[1] has mentioned the name of Tana Taranga and described him as one of the principal musicians of the Court of Akbar. Blochmann[2] in his English Translation of Ain-I-Akbari, mentions the name of Bilas Khan, Faqirullah[3] has mentioned the name of Surat Sen another son of Tansen in addition to the above two. Regarding his other son we find his name being mentioned as Sharat Sen[4+5] and as Hamir Sen[6]. Faqirullah has based the Genealogical chart of Tansen with the help of Bhagwan, blind Pakhawaj player, who always used to accompany Tansen and he has written about Hamir Sen[7] who seems to have been fourth son of Tansen. Karam Imam[8] has written that Tansen had a daughter whose name was Saraswati Devi who was married to Misri Singh (Naubat Khan) son of Raja Samokhan Singh. However Brahaspati Ji[9] is of the view that Wazir Khan's (Rampur) fore fathers have fabricated the story of Tansen having a daughter. From some legends of Akbar's time such as when Tansen sang Deepak Raga, his body started having blisters and it is said that subsequently Tansen's daughter, Saraswati Devi, saved her father from dying by singing Raga Mega which brought down the temperature of environments. Misri Singh and his descendants who were all instrumentalists and accompanists, were not given any reference and we do not find their names in the books of that period. It is Niyamat Khan who is credited as having made Veena as a solo instrument during the reign of

1. Abul-Fazal, 'Ain-I-Akbari, p. 681.
2. *Ibid.*
3. Faqirullah, 'Rag Darpan', p. 130.
4. Roy Chaudhuri Birendra Kishore, 'Indian Music and Mian Tansen, p. 21.
5. Roy Chaudhuri Bimal Kant, 'Bhartiya Sangeet Kosh', p. 168.
6. Brahaspati Acharya, 'Musalman Aur Bhartiya Sangeet', p. 105.
7. *Ibid.*
8. Hakim Karam Imam, 'Mudunnul Mausiqui', p. 34.
9. Acharya Brahaspati, 'Dhrupada Aur Uska Vikas', p. 208.

Mohammad Shah Rangila (Reign A.D. 1719-1748) and he was a descendant of Misri Singh, it indicates, that Tansen had a daughter. Some musicians now give the reason that authors of sixteenth and seventeenth Century seem to have avoided writing much about the women. For that matter they give the reason that not much was written about Akbar's daughter, Maherunissa and it is difficult to find as to whom she was married and thus, if Saraswati Devi, did not get any reference in any book of that period, it should not be surprising.

Surat Sen was son of Tansen and his descendants mostly settled at Jaipur.[1] He was a practical singer and musician and knew principles and theory of music while his brothers were *atai* musicians. His sons were Suhir Sen[2], Mohan Sen[3].

Tan Tarang Khan was the elder son of Tansen and his name has been included among the distinguished singers of Akbar's Court[4]. His remaining life, after Akbar's reign is not known, however some of his Dhrupada's are available. Faqirullah[5] has mentioned him as *atai*. He was given the rank of Gandharva.[6]

Bilas Khan was the youngest son of Tansen. He was the Chief Court Musician of Jehangir (reign A.D. 1605-1627) who was great lover of music like his father Akbar. In Badshahnama, Abul-Fazal has written that Bilas Khan was younger brother of Tan-Tarang Khan and was in Jehangir's Darbar. Bilas Khan was specialist in the Dhrupada of *Sudha Vani* and in the Instrumental Music of Rabab. Bilas Khan and his disciples kept up the

1. Roy Chaudhuri, Birendra Kishore, 'Indian Music and Mian Tansen', p. 29.
2. Arshi, I.A.; Op. Cit. 'Hindustan Ke Chand Mashoor Mausiqui' (Article), Aaj Kal, August, 1956. (Faqirulla Rag Darpen Hindi Translation,) p. 130.
3. Ibid., p. 136.
4. Roy Chaudhuri, Bimal Kant, 'Bhartiya Sangeet Kosh', p. 168.
5. Blochman, 'Ain-I-Akbari, p. 680
6. Faqirullah, 'Rag Darpan', Translation Dewvedi, p. 130.

tradition of playing Rabab and singing Dhrupada only for its sanctified or distinguished association with Tansen. Some musicologists believe that Bilaskhani Todi was invented by Bilas Khan[1]. However Brahaspati[2] is of the view that it was some Vilas Khan Qawwal who invented it. There are certain Dhrupadas of Bilas Khan available. Bilas Khan had two sons named as Uday Sen and Dayal Sen and one daughter and among his disciples was Misri Khan Dhari.

Hamir Sen was a renowned Kalawant during Aurangzeb's period and was born some time during Akbar's time. He died at the age of eighty.[3]

Rang Khan was a student of Tansen and a Kalawant of high reputation in Shah Jehan's Court.

Bakht Khan :- He was also a student of Mian Tansen. Faqirullah states: "Although I have seen him, I have not heard him, but my musician friends spoke highly of his art. He died at the age of fifty six. Basant Kalawant, who was his disciple, was a good singer and I had an opportunity of listening to him. From his songs I could guess about the talents of his Guru".[4]

Uday Sen :- He was the son of Bilas Khan and was an accomplished Vocalist and Rabab player. His son, Karim Sen, was married to his brother Dayal Sen's daughter.

Misri Khan Dhari :- He was one of the disclipes of Bilas Khan. He went to Bengal with Sultan Shuja Khan. His compositions were of good quality and were very popular. He was eighty years old when Faqirullah wrote about him[5]. His Dhrupadas are still available.

---

1. Arshi, I.A.; 'Hindustan Ke Chand Mashoor Mausiqui' (Article), Aaj Kal, August, 1956.
2. Acharya Brahaspati, 'Sangeet Chintmani', p. 484.
3. Faqirullah, 'Rag Darpan', p. 102.
4. Faqirullah, 'Rag Darpan', p.137
5. Ibid. 'Raag Darpan Dewvedi', p. 136

Lal Khan (Gun Samundar):- Tansen was very much impressed with the musical talents of Lal Khan Kalawant who got him married to Bilas Khan's daughter. Lal Khan was Court Musician of Jehangir (Reign A.D. 1605-1627) and an outstanding musician in the Court of Shahjehan (Reign A.D. 1627-1658). Jehangir has written that Lal Khan died at the age of sixty five in third year of his reign i.e. 1608 A.D.[1] On the other hand it is mentioned in Badshahnama that Lal Khan got the title of Gun Samundar in 1630 from Shahjehan and he died in 1652 A.D. at Agra.[2] His style of singing resembled Tansen's singing, which he acquired from Tansen as well as from Bilas Khan. He was unparalleled in Dhrupada singing. He had four sons Khushal Khan, Bisram Khan, Rasbin Khan and the fourth son's name is not known.

Sudhir Sen :- Sudhir Sen was the son of Surat Sen.[3] We also find the name of Mohan Sen[4] as son of Surat Sen. Sohil Sen was a protege of Shah-Shuja, son of Shahjehan and was an Ustad in Music. He died in Bengal. His son Sudhir Sen, was not as good a singer as he, but he was a good poet. When Faqirullah wrote the book he was alive at that time.[5]

Khushal Khan and Bisram Khan were both sons of Lal Khan. Khushal Khan was a very good singer and was best singer among his brothers. He was a favourite singer of Shahjehan and used to include his name in his compositions.[6] Faqirullah[7] has stated, "Khushal Khan was in Shahjehan's Court and is still alive. He has close contact with Emperor Aurangzeb. May God give him a long life as he has no parallel among the Kalawants". Bisram Khan

1. The Tuzuk-I-Jehangiri of Jehangir, Vol. I, p. 150.
2. Badshahnama, Raza Library Rampur.
3. Faqirullah, 'Raag Darpan', p. 136.
4. Roy Chaudhuri, Bimal Kant, p. 168.
5. Faqirullah, 'Rag Darpan', Dewvedi, p. 136.
6. Acharya Brahaspati, 'Musalman Aur Bhartiya Sangeet', p. 76.
7. Faqirullah, 'Rag Darpan', p. 130.

also used to sing like his brother and there is a well known story associated with these musicians. It is said that Aurangzeb wanted Murshid Quli Khan to accompany him to South, but Shahjehan wanted him to stay with Dara. Khushal Khan along with his brother Bisram Khan took Rupees one lakh from Amir-Ul-Umra for getting the order to Murshid Quli Khan signed by Emperor. The signatures on order were obtained on the occasion of Nauroze when a large musical gathering was arranged. They sat at a distance of ten yards from the emperor's throne and sang Rag Todi. Shahjehan was very fond of this particular raag. Khushal Khan and Bisram Khan sang a Dhrupada in this raag which totally absorbed the emperor. Finding the occasion suitable, these two brothers gave a hint to Amir-Ul-Umra who placed the document before the Emperor, who signed it without looking at it, and thus Murshid Quli Khan was sent with Aurangazeb. Later when Shahjehan came to know about this intrigue, he was angry and dismissed both the musicians from the Court. They both became the Court musicians of Aurangzeb. Khushal Khan was given the title of Gun Samundar by Aurangzeb.[1] He was the best musician in his court in 1665. Bisram Khan died in 1671.[2]

Rasbin Khan :- He was another brother of Khushal Khan and was a Court Musician of Shahjehan and Aurangzeb. He was in Auragnzeb's Court till 1667-1683 and after that it is beleived that Aurangzeb banned music from his Court.[3]

Bhupat Khan :- He was the son of Bisram Khan and was also Court Musician of Aurangzeb. He was given MATMI KHELAT along with Khushal Khan in 1671, when his father Bisram Khan died.[4] After Bhupat Khan the descendants of Lal Khan are not traceable.

---

1. Acharya Brahaspati, 'Musalman Aur Bhartiya Sangeet, p. 77.
2. 'Aurangzeb Nama', Vol. II p. 32.
3. *Ibid.*, Vol. II, p. 32.
4. 'Aurangzeb Nama', p. 32.

Karim Sen :- Karim Sen was grandson of Bilas Khan and son of Uday Sen. He was married to the daughter of his uncle, Dayal Sen, and had two sons, Sudhir Sen and Rajras Khan.[1]

Subsequently Rajras Khan's line is not traceable till Sukh Sen and Rahim Sen, although Bimal Kant Roy Chaudhuri[2] has shown Masit Khan was the son of Rajras Khan. This statement is doubtful since Masit Khan was son of Feroz Khan and grandson of Khusroo Khan[3] , who was younger brother of Niyamat Khan Sadarang and belonged to Misri Singh's line.

Misri Singh :- He is supposed to be the son of Raja Samokhan Singh and is said to have been a Court Musician in Akbar's Court. It is beleived that he married Saraswati Devi, the daughter of Tansen. He was a celeberated Veena Player.[4]

His descendants were regarded as the authorities in the Instrumental Music of "*Veena*" and used to sing Dhrupada in '*Dagar Vani*' and '*Khander Vani*'.[5] Bimal Kant Chaudhuri[6] has shown his descendants till Niyamat Khan. Since no reference regarding any of these musicians in any of the texts of those time is found, the genealogical chart is reproduced as given by Bimal Kant Roy Chaudhuri.

Niyamat Khan :- He was son of Nirmal Khan[7] or Lal Khan[8]. He was the Court Musician of Bahadur Shah (Reign A.D. 1707-1712), Jahandar Shah (Reign A.D. 1712-1713), Mohammad Shah Rangila (Reign A.D. 1713-1748).[9] Dargah Quli Khan, who visited Delhi in 1738 A.D., has written a

---

1. Roy Chaudhuri, Bimal Kant, 'Bhartiya Sangeet Kosh', p. 168.
2. *Ibid.*
3. Acharya Sudarshan, 'Sangeet Sudarshan', p. 26.
4. Roy Chaudhuri, Birendra Kishore, 'Indian Music & Mian Tansen', p. 7.
5. Roy Chaudhuri Birendra Kishore, 'Indian Music & Mian Tansen', p. 7.
6. 'Mirati Aftabnuma', p. 390 B.
7. Ibid.
8. Roy Chaudhuri Bimal Kant, 'Bhatiya Sangeet Kosh', p. 168.
9. Acharya Brahaspati, 'Musalman Aur Bhartiya Sangeet', p. 78.

book, Muraqqa-E-Delhi (!738), after Nadir Shah had invaded Delhi. He has given a description of Niyamat Khan. He says :- "His presence in North India is God's great gift. He is matchless in the art of music. He has a remarkable capacity for composing various styles of songs. At present he is considered the master of the contemporary musicians. He does not concede to anybody's request for singing except the king's. His supreme proficiency in playing *Been* shows that no such *Beenkar* was ever born before him. He has a magic in his voice. He goes to the Dargahs of saints and sometimes also holds musical sittings at his place, where it appears as if the whole of Delhi is thronging"[1]

According to Miraat-E-Aftab-Numa, Niyamat Khan used to compose Dhrupada, Khayal, Tarana and other styles with great maturity, freshness and colourfulness. He acquired the art of music from a Tatari Qawwal, Bengali Natwar and Devdatta Kavishvar. He was honoured and respected in the Court of Jahandarshah. King Mohammad Shah Rangila brought him up and was his great admirer. Niyamat Khan died in the later part of Mohammad Shah's rule.[2] He received the title of Shah Sadarang in the Darbar of Mohammad Shah Rangila and is ranked the second great musician of India after Mian Tansen. He was the high priest of Mohammad Shah's Darbar. He also created the classical Khayal and founded the famous Kawwal *Gharana* through his disciples, whom he taught classical Khayal.[3] He is also credited as having made *Veena* a Solo Instrument because till his time *"Veena"* was only an accompanying instrument. His prominent disciples were Qasim Ali, Panna Lal and Kamaal Bai.

Khusroo Khan :- He was the younger brother of Niyamat Khan and is credited with having invented the Sitar.[4] Nizami states that one of his speciality was that he could

1. Dargah Quli Khan's, Muraqqa-E-Delhi.
2. 'Mirati Aftabnuma', p. 293A.
3. Roy Chaudhuri Birendra Kishore, 'Indian Music and Mian Tansen', p. 28.
4. Acharya Brahaspati, 'Musalman Aur Bhartiya Sangeet', p. 79.

play this particular type of instrument for a very long duration in different ways. He possessed an instrument with three strings which was unusual at that time. On that instrument he could play all Ragas and Raginis. Possibly this instrument could be the fore runner of the modern instrument, Sitar. He had also innovated a number of new Ragas and Raginis.[1]

Feroz Khan :- He was son of Khusroo Khan and father of Masit Khan and was married to the daughter of Sadarang.[2] He was disciple of Niyamat Khan and was trained in the same way as Niyamat Khan and was known as Adarang. He was a very good singer of his time. In one of his Dhrupada, he has said that when a man gets a chance to sing, he should start singing by taking the name of Sadarang first. It shows that he was a disciple of Niyamat Khan.[3] His compositions are available wherein he has mentioned the name of Mohammad Shah Rangila and Alamgir Sahni (reign A.D. 1748-1759).

Mahawat Khan :- He was son of Niyamat Khan and was known as Manrang and has written *HORI*[4] in honour of his father and Dhrupada[5] in honour of Mohammad Shah Rangila. He had two sons, Charju Khan and Jeewan Khan.

Charju Khan :- Charju Khan was a good *Been* player and Dhrupada singer. He had three sons Pyar Khan, Basat Khan and Jafar Khan and one daughter through whom Bahadur Hussain Khan was born.

Jeewan Khan :- He was also a very good *Been* player and Dhrupada singer. Bahadur Khan and Haider Khan[6] were his two sons.

---

1. Nizami K.H. 'Purani Delhi Ke Halaat'.
2. Sudarshan Acharya, 'Sangeet Sudarshan', p. 26.
3. Ragmala, p. 123.
4. Imam Karam Hakim, Mudunul Mausiqui, p. 32.
5. Ibid., p. 33.
6. Acharya Brahaspati, 'Sangeet Chintamani', p. 604.

Pyar Khan, Basat Khan & Jafar Khan were three brothers of great reputation in playing *Rabab* and singing *Dhrupada*. Nirmal Shah, their cousin brother, was a great *Been* player.

All these musicians made Varanasi their home as they left Delhi in their early years. They were attached to the Court of Lucknow. Jafar Khan was a great instrumentalist in Rabab. His instrument had its lower part covered by the skin parchment and strings used in it were made of the 'Guts'. Its display had no parallel in the *'Jod'* tyle and *Tar-Paran*. Being closely related to Nirmal Shah, they had to compete with each other in the Court of Lucknow and Kashi. In order to equal the charms of the Been which was displayed with great skill and sweetness by Nirmal Shah, Jafar Khan invented the instrument of *Sur-Sringar*. Pyar Khan specialised in this instrument after Jafar Khan added some fascinating ornamentations in the style of its display.[1] Jafar Khan had four sons who were Kazam Ali, Sadiq Ali, Ahmed Ali and Nisar Ali and his disciples were Bahadur Sen and Maharaja Vishwanath Singh of Rewa. Pyar Khan adopted his sister's son, Bahadur Hussain whom he trained. Basat Khan had three sons who were Ali Mohammad, Mohammad Ali and Reyasat Ali and his disciples were Kasim Ali (Sarod), Niyamatulah Khan (Sarod), Raja Ftar Kumar Thakur and Paul Chowdhary of Ranaghat.[2]

Haider Khan & Bahadur Khan :- Haider Khan and Bahadur Khan were sons of Jeewan Khan and cousin brothers of Jafar Khan. They were both *Ustads* in music.[3] Nawab Ali Naki Shah (Dewan of Wazid Ali Shah) was their student. Haider Khan is the founder of *Betiya Gharana*. Gadadhar Chakravarti of Vishnupur was also student of Bahadur Khan.[4] Bakar Khan was another son of Jeewan Khan as shown by Bimal Kant Roy Chaudhuri.[5]

---

1. Roy Chaudhuri, Birendra Kishore, "Indian Music and Mian Tansen', pp. 21-22.
2. Chaudhuri, Bimal Kant, 'Bhartiya Sangeet Kosh', p. 16.
3. Imam Karam Hakim -- 'Mudunul Mausiqui' p. 33.
4. Roy Chaudhuri Bimal Kant, p. 16.
5. Ibid.

Bahadur Hussain Khan :- He was adopted child of Pyar Khan and was his nephew. He had most of his training under him. He along with Amir Khan, his son-in-law, were founders of Rampur *Gharana*. He concentrated more on instrumental music and had such a charming style of playing that people used to say that his fingers were made of diamonds. Not only the lovers of classical music, but even uninitiated laymen were overwhelmed with rapturous joy by the sound of his instrumental display. He was also known as "Niya-U-Dola".[1] Among his disciples were Nawab Haider Ali Khan of Rampur, Panna Lal Bajapayee (Sitar); Inayat Hussain and Mohammad Hussain Khan (Been); Buniyade Hussain Khan (Dhrupada & Khayal); Gulam Nabi Khan (Sori), Majru Khan (Sarod) and Ahmed Hussain (Been). Panna Lal Bajapayee used to play Sitar with two mizrabs and was a very good Sitarist in Banaras.[2]

Turab Ali, Umrao Khan and Mohammad Ali Khan were all sons of Haider Khan. Umrao Khan was a renowned Beenkar of his time. It was he who invented the instrument "*Sur-bahar*" and taught Gulam Mohammad Khan its mode of display. His other brothers were also great Beenkars. Varanasi saw many friendly duels of instrumental music between Pyar Khan and Umrao Khan in *Sur-Sringar* and Been.[3] Umrao Khan had two sons Amir Khan and Rahim Khan and his disciples were Kutub Baksh, Gulam Mohammad Khan and his son Sajad Mohammad Khan and Hasmat Jang (Nawab of Banda).[4]

Ali Mohammad, Mohammad Ali and Reyasat Ali were all sons of Basat Khan. Ali Mohammad Khan was the *Sur-Sringar* player of repute and Mohammad Ali Khan was vocalist and *Rababi* who settled at Gaya after the sepoy Mutiny. After the death of their cousin brother Sedak Ali

1. Personal Communications with Prof. Radhika Mohan Moitra.
2. Personal Communications with Shri Bimal Kant Roy Chaudhuri.
3. Roy Chaudhuri Birendra Kishore, 'Indian Music and Mian Tansen', p. 22.
4. Roy Chaudhuri Bimal Kant, p. 172.

Khan, Ali Mohammad Khan, the eldest son of Basat Khan, was appointed by the Raja of Varanasi as the Chief Musician of his Court. Ali Mohammad Khan was a very liberal minded musician and used to play on his *Sur-Sringar* before his disciples without any reservations. He had profound knowledge of *Ragas* and could develop any *Raga* for hours. He trained up Panna Lal Jain, Arjundas Vaidya, a practitioner of Ayurvedic Medicines and Gaya Prasad Misra in *Sur-Sringar*. Sayed Mir Nasir Khan of Jullunder was his most accomplished disciples in *Sur-Sringar* He also imparted lessons on the Vocal Music of *Dhrupada* and Instrumental Music on *Beena* and *Sur-Sringar* to the great *Beena* player, Wazir Khan Saheb of Rampur, who was related very closely to him. Ali Mohammad Khan taught the famous Bengali musician, late Hari Narayan Mukherjee, many *Dhrupadas* and *Sargams* Tara Prasad Ghosh, who was well known in Calcutta for his charities towards musicians, learnt many songs from him.[1] Mohammad Ali Khan, the younger brother of Ali Mohammad Khan who used to stay at Gaya, frequently visited his elder brother for lessons on Rabab. Both these brothers outshone all other famous musicians of that period who used to visit Varanasi.[2] Mohammad Ali Khan had one son whose name was Ali Baksh Khan. Ali Baksh Khan trained the following[3] musicians :- Nawab Hamid Ali of Rampur, Shokat Ali Khan *(Rabab & Sur-Sringar)* Behari Lal Panda of Gaya, Kanayi Lal Tendi of Gaya, Girija Shankar Chakarvorti, Nawab Sabat Ali Khan (Chamman Sahib), Thakur Nawab Ali Khan and Salamat Khan.[4]

Kazam Ali, Sadiq Ali, Ahmed Ali and Nisar Ali [5] were sons of Jafar Khan. Sadiq Ali and Nisar Ali became attached to the Court of the Raja of Varanasi. Sadiq Ali was a great musicologist and excelled in Rabab and could also

1. Roy Chaudhuri, Birendra Kishore, "Indian Music and Mian Tansen', pp. 23-24.
2. Roy Chaudhuri, Bimal Kant, 'Bhartiya Sangeet Kosh', p. 170.
3. Ibid.
4. Roy Chaudhuri, Bimal Kant, Bhartiya Sangeet Kosh', p. 168.
5. Imam Karam Hakim, 'Mudunul Mausiqui', p. 32.

play Beena very efficiently. He was also intimately associated with the Sanskrit Scholars of Varanasi and was an erudite scholar in Sanskrit and Persian languages. The Raja had a great respect for him. It is said that Sadiq Ali Khan had no equal in the improvisation of '*Ladi-Jod*', '*Lad-Guthao*'. In the *Tar-paran* he could beat any *Mridanga* player. He lived like a saint and had a religious temperament. He could not tolerate the music of lighter moods. He taught *Rabab* only to his younger brothers. But he had many disciples of *Dhrupada* and in the Instrumental Music of *Beena* and *Sitar* The most outstanding of them was the Sitar players, Bajpayee Ji., Mahesh Chandra Sarkar and Methailallji were his disciples in *Beena*. Sri Ramakrishna Paramahansa Dev, when he went to Varanasi on pilgrimage, listened to the *Beena* of Mahesh Sarkar and was absorbed in Samadhi.[1] Nisar Ali had following disciples:- Wazir Khan of Rampur (*Been, Rabab & Sur-Sringar*), Panna Lal Bajpayee (*Sitar*) Jeewan Lal Maharaj and Ved Arjun Das.[2]

Amir Khan and Rahim Khan :- Amir Khan and Rahim Khan were both sons of Umrao Khan.[3] Brahaspati Ji[4] has reported that Amir Khan was son-in-law of Bahadur Hussain Khan while Birendra Kishore Roy Chaudhuri[5] reports that Amir Khan was son-in-law of Kazam Ali. The Rampur *Gharana* was founded by Amir Khan and Bahadur Hussain Khan.[6] Amir Khan was a very good *Beenkar* and on the other hand, had a very melodious voice and although originally an instrumentalist, his concentration was on Vocal Music. In Rampur *Darbar* he seldom played on *Beena* in presence of Bahadur Hussain Khan. He used to sing in the Darbar Vocal, *Alap, Dhrupadas* and *Dhamars* Amir Khan was famous in the use of *Meend* and *Murans* and some *Alankars* which sounded like *Murki* and *Firat*.

1. Roy Chaudhuri, Bimal Kant, Tansen, p. 23.
2. Ibid.
3. Acharya Brahaspati, 'Musalman Aur Bhartiya Sangeet', p. 87
4. ibid.
5. Roy Chaudhuri, Birendra Kishore 'Indian Music and Mian Tansen', p. 32.
6. Roy Chaudhuri, Bimal Kant, 'Bhartiya Sangeet Kosh', p. 34.

All the musicians who came to Rampur during this time became the disciples of either Bahadur Hussain or Amir Khan.[1] They were the Court Musicians of Nawab Wazid Ali Shah. In 1864 they came to Nawab Kalabey Khan. Haider Ali Khan, who was step-brother of Nawab Kalabey Ali Khan of Rampur, had his musical training from Bahadur Hussain Khan, Amir Khan, Basat Khan and Sadiq Ali Khan.[2] Rahim Khan was younger brother of Amir Khan and had a good hand[3], and gave training to Feda Hussain Khan *(Rabab & Sarod)*, Buniyad Hussain *(Dhrupada & Hori)* and Mohammad Hussain *(Been)*. Amir Khan had two sons who were Wazir Khan and Feyali Khan (Feyad Ali).[4]

Wazir Khan :- He was son of Amir Khan and was born in 1861. He was most famous *Been* Player of Rampur during his time. He passed away in 1926. His father and Bahadur Hussain Khan both passed away when he was just ten to eleven years of age. Nawab Haider Ali Khan, who was born in 1846, gave him training in music. Also he had his initial training from his father in *Beena* and in *Sur-Sringar* from Bahadur Hussain Khan. He had his training from his uncle Rahim Khan also but subsequently Nawab Haider Ali Khan, as his guardian, developed his extraordinary musical genius. He also learnt *Dhrupada, Dhamar* and was both a melodious vocalist and a great instrumentalist. Nawab Chamman Sahib was his colleague. He built the musical carrier of the following outstanding musicians:- Allaudin Khan *(Sarod)*, Mehdi Hussain Khan *(Dhrupada & Khayal)*, Mushtaq Hussain Khan *(Khayal)*; Pramathanath, *(Rudra Veena)*; Jadabendra Mahapatra *(Sur-Bahar)*; Pandit Bhatkhandeji (the great musicologist); Abdhar Rahim *(Sitar)*; Tara Prasad Ghosh *(Dhrupada)*; Nawab Hamid Ali and Nasir Ali *(Surbahar & Sitar)* In his youth, he was in Calcutta and developed musical talent of many Bangalees and helped in developing Classical Music in Vengal.[5]

---

1. Roy Chaudhuri Birendra Kishore, 'Indian Music & Mian Tansen', p. 32.
2. Acharya Brahaspati, 'Musalman Aur Bhartiya Sangeet', pp. 96-97.
3. Ibid., p. 87.
4. Roy Chaudhuri Bimal Kant, 'Bhartiya Sangeet Kosh', p. 170.
5. Roy Chaudhuri Birendra Kishore, 'Indian Music & Mian Tansen', pp. 34-35.

Nawab Haider Ali Khan :- He was step brother of Kalabey Ali Khan and was born in 1846. He was a very good music teacher, poet and knew many languages. Rampur state, during his time, had a galaxy of musicians. Haider Ali Khan had two sons Chamman Sahib and Jani Sahib and both had music training from him. Chamman Sahib was Guru and the friend of Vishnu Narayan Bhatkhanday, the great musicologist, who learnt about Ragas from him. Chamman Sahib has written Falsafey-Museke and his brother wrote Nagmey Sadate. Their mother, Lali, was also a good singer and Ganpat Rao of Gwalior was the son of Chanderbaga, sister of Lali. Bhatkhande College of Music, Lucknow, which is now the Centre of Bhatkhande University, got tremendous support from Nawab Hamid Ali Khan of Rampur and Nawab Chamman Sahib, who helped this great institution, both financially and also with the precious teachings of the Rampur *Gharana*.

Nazir Khan, Nasir Khan & Sagir Khan were sons of Wazir Khan. Sagir Khan went to Pakistan at partition. Sagir Khan did build the musical talents of Khemendar Mohan Thakur, Prakash Gosh, Pani Mukhopadyaya and Birendra Kishore Roy Chaudhuri before going to Pakistan, where he did not take much interest in music.[1]

Chamman Khan, Dabir Khan and Dildar Khan were all sons of Nazir Khan. Out of all these brothers, Dabir Khan, who was born in 1902, was one of the top musicians in Calcutta and built the musical career of the following musicians :- Kalidas Sanyal, Khemendar Mohan Thakur, Jai Krishna Sanyal, Jatender Mohan Sen Gupta, Jotshi Chander Choudhury, Dr. Trina Prohit, Dr. Dena Rai, Nand Gopal Vishwanath, Vipin Chander Das, Veenapani Mukhopadaya, Virinder Vandhopadaya, Virinder Mukhopadaya, Mamta Mitra, Maya Mitra, Maya Rai, Raja Rai, Radhika

1. Dr. Chobey Sushil Kumar, 'Sangeet Ke Gharane Ki Charcha', p. 58.

Mohan Moitra, Shalinder Mohan Vandopadaya, Shamal Chathopadaya, Santosh Kumar Vandopadaya and Birendra Kishore Roy Choudhuri.[1] The later was very loved disciple of Dabir Khan. Birendra Kishore Roy Chaudhuri has passed away a couple of years ago.[2]

Maseet Khan :- He was the grandson of Khusroo Khan and son of Feroz Khan. Niyamat Khan was his maternal grand father. Maseet Khan had his training in Sitar from his brother, Feroz Khan. *Maseet Khani Baj* of *Vilambit* which is also known as *Delhi-Ka-Baj* is famous after his name as he used it first. During his time no *Jod* used to be played on Sitar, only *Gat* and *Toda* used to be played. The Sitar in its present shape and form owes much to the pioneering work done by Maseet Khan. A strict follower of *Dhrupada* tradition Maseet Khan composed his *Gats* in the four principal movements of the *Dhrupada*; i.e. *Sthayi*, *Antara*, *Samchari* and *Abhog*. Maseet Khan laid great emphasis on the importance of *Bols* played with right hand which were crystallised into a definite shape and the *Bols* were standardised. These *Gats* having a positive form with *Asthai* and *Antara* fully rendered, were followed by *Todas* in *Vilambit Laya*. The *Todas* were composed on the basis of *Paranas* of *Pakhawaj* or *Tabla*. Maseet Khan taught Sitar to his sister's son Dulhe Khan. Sukh Sen, Nur Sen and Bahadur Sen, were his own sons.

Dulhe Khan :- Dulhe Khan was daughters son of Feroz Khan. He was master of *Beena* and *Dhrupad* and had his Sitar training from his maternal uncle, Maseet Khan. He remained for some time with the Naresh of Gwalior. Dulhe Khan had one daughter, who was married to Rahim Sen and his son was Haider Khan.

Rahim Sen :- Rahim Sen was son-in-law of Dulhe Khan and was a descendant of Bilas Khan. His father's name was Sukh Sen. His grand father and father both were Ustads of Dhrupada.[3] Many authors report that Rahim Sen was

1. Roy Chaudhuri Bimal Kant, 'Bhartiya Sangeet Kosh', p. 172.
2. Chobey Dr. Sushil Kumar, 'Sangeet Ke Gharano Ke Charcha', p. 58.
3. Acharya Sudarshan, 'Sangeet Sudarshan', p. 27.

son of Maseet Khan,[1] but Sudarshan Acharya has written that Maseet Khan was a descendant of Misri Singh, while as Rahim Sen was descendant of Bilas Khan[2], probably in the line of Rajras Khan. Since Sudarshan Acharya was a student of Rahim Sen's son, Amrit Sen, his statement seems to be authentic regarding the ancestors of Rahim Sen. Rahim Sen is credited with having brought Sitar to the level of *Beena* which was a most played and liked instrument of that time. Rahim Sen along with his son, Amrit Sen, introduced *Veena*, *Dhrupada* & *Khayal*, all three into Sitar and used to play first *Jod* and then *Gat*, *Toda* and then *Fikrey*. In it *Jod* is from *Veena*, *Alap*, *Gat* and *Toda* from *Dhrupada* and *Asthai* from *Khayal*. Some things in their Sitar were such which could not be sung or played on *Veena*. He taught Sitar to many, out of them, Hussain Khan Ji, his younger brother was best.

Haider Khan :- He was son of Dulhe Khan and his sons were Wazir Khan, Almu Khan, Mamu Khan, Salawat Khan and Alawat Khan. Wazir Khan was married to the daughter of Rahim Sen. All these brothers learnt from Amrit Sen and mostly lived with him. Among these brothers Almu Khan and Mamu Khan became good musicians. Haider Khan was a *Dhrupada* singer and had good knowledge of music. Besides *Dhrupada*, he had a good knowledge of Sitar and *Veena* and gave training in music to many of his students. At his death Amrit Sen said, "The music school of our home has died today". He died at ripe age of 106 years, some moments after explaining about a *Dhrupada* to his one son who had asked about it.

Amrit Sen :- Amrit Sen was elder son of Rahim Sen and had two brothers whose names were Niyamat Sen and Lal Sen. His sister was married to Wazir Khan son of Haider Baksh. Niyamat Sen learnt Sitar from Amrit Sen and other brother had the training under his father, Rahim Sen.

---

1. Acharya Brahaspati, 'Musalman Aur Bhartiya Sangeet', p. 38.
2. Acharya Sudarshan, 'Sangeet Sudarshan', p. 27.

Niyamat Sen was very good in Sitar and had a delicate and sweet hand for Sitar, but died at a very young age. Lal Sen developed certain defects in his hands after eating certain substance and could not persue the Sitar subsequently. Amrit Sen had no son but had two daughters who were married to Amir Khan's sons. He adopted Nihal Khan who was son of Wazir Khan. Amrit Sen was born in 1813 in Janjar. In 1857 Nawab of Janjar was hanged and so Amrit Sen came to Delhi for some time. From Delhi he was taken by Shiv Dan Singh, Naresh of Alwar. Due to political differences of Shiv Dan Singh with English, Amrit Sen had to leave Alwar and came back to Delhi. Both Gwalior Naresh Jiyajee, and Jaipur Naresh Ram Singh Ji, wanted him in their courts. Since Ram Singh's man came first, so he went to Jaipur and settled there permanently. In 1893 after marrying his two daughters to two sons of Amir Khan, he became ill and died in the same year at the age of 80 years.

Amrit Sen and Hafiz Khan :- He seldom used to teach Sitar to persons outside his family but has taught to Sudarshan Acharya Sastri and Nawab of Janjar. Amir Khan was best Sitar player after Amrit Sen among all his pupils.

Amrit Sen was a very good *Dhrupada* singer in *Gouhar Vani* although he never used to sing in the public, since his father had advised him not to sing or play except Sitar in public. By the age of ten years, Amrit Sen used to play Sitar along with his father on stages and by 13 years he started giving solo performances. He had named his Sitar as Mani Ram. It is believed that Rahim Sen and Amrit Sen played Sitar so beautifully that subsequently their melody in playing resulted in death of other instruments and *Dhrupada* in their family.

Amir Khan and Nihal Khan :- Both were sons of Wazir Khan who was married to sister of Amrit Sen. They all lived together along with Amrit Sen, Haider Baksh and sons of Haider Baksh. Nihal Sen was adopted son of Amrit Sen and subsequently took his place in Jaipur. Amir Khan was born at Janjar and had his education in Sitar from Amrit Sen and also from his maternal grand father, Rahim Sen. His father, Wazir Khan, was a good *Beenkar* and his grand father, Haider Baksh, was a *Dhrupada* singer. Amir Khan was a very good Sitar player and had a deep knowledge of music also. Amir Khan initially remained more with Alwar Naresh than with Ram Singh of Jaipur, then in Gwalior with Jiyaji Maharaj and was Guru of Madav Rao Maharaj, who was son of Jiyaji. He had three sons Feda Hussain, Fazal Hussain and the name of 3rd son could not be found.

Fazal Hussain died at a very young age. His two sons were married to two daughters of Amrit Sen. Amir Khan passed away in 1915.

Ustad Barkatullah Khan :- He was initially a *Pakhawaj* player but became disciple of Amir Khan and learnt Sitar from him. Ustad Barkatullah Khan although a *Pakhawaj* Player acquired a mastery over the Sitar and became the most brilliant Sitar player of his time in Senia *Gharana.* He was a Court Musician of Patiala and Mysore. His disc record of a *Gat* in *Bhupkalyan* gives us some idea of the authentic Senia Baj. Barkatullah Khan Ji taught Sitar to Ustad Ashiq Ali Khan, who was accomplished Sitar player of his time.

Ustad Mushtaq Ali Khan :- Ustad Mushtaq Ali Khan is son of Ustad Ashiq Ali Khan and had his training both under his grand father and his father. He is a renowned Sitar player of Senia *Gharana.* He is a firm believer of the rules of the Sitar technique of Senia *Gharana* and maintains the purity of his traditions. He has taught Sitar to following of his accomplished disciples :- Arun Kumar Chattopadaya, Ashok Gosh, Nikhil Bandopadaya, Nitai Chander Basu, Nirmal Kant Lahidi Chowdhary and Debu Choudhuri. Out of his pupils Pandit Debu Choudhuri has followed the Senia Baj and popularised Sitar in many parts of the world and is famous for his clarity and sweetness in playing Sitar.

CHAPTER IV

'DHRUPADA' ITS EVOLUTION AND THE COMPOSITIONS OF SENIA'S

The word *Dhrupada* is a combination of two Sanskrit words viz. *Dhruva* and *Pada*. *Dhruva* means structure fixed or rigid and *Pada* means word or syllable. The word *Dhrupada* or *Dhruvapada*, therefore, means a composition in which the *Padas* or words are set in a definite structure or pattern. *Dhrupada* is also known as "strict style" and it is so with the *Dhrupada* style. *Dhrupada* consists of four rhythmical lines without any definite prosodial length of words or syllables. *Dhruva* singifies the introductory stanza or recurring verse of a poem or song repeated as a refrain.[1]

The history of evolution of Dhrupada is usually traced to the Vedic times. In Vedic times two classes of music existed which were *samagana* and the *sametara*. The *Samagana* was musical rendering of a Rgvedic text and *Sametara* was essentially the music of the commoners, though it could also be sung at the time of religious sacrifices. The *Sametara* music was thought to be less prestigious in comparison to *Samagana* In course of time particularly in post Vedic period the *Samagana* lost its ground and the *Sametara* with its sub-varieties like *gatha*, *narasansi*, *Uktha* etc. became fashionable. With the passing of time another form of music which was known as *gandharva* (celestial) came into lime light and *Sametara* lost its ground. There is extensive mention of it in Natya-Sastra

1. Abul Fazal, 'Ain-I-Akbari', Translation by Colonel H.S. Jarrett, p. 266.
2. Acharya Brahaspati 'Vagyeyakaron Ki Parampara Aur Dhrupada Ke Visayon Ka Srota', p. 28.

written by Bharata. Besides *Gandharva*, we get evidence from Natya-Sastra, that a non-gandharvic form of music also existed at that time which was in the form of *dhruvas*, the stage songs. *dhruvas* were employed to enhance the effect of the different situations occurring in a dramatic performance. Since no mention of *Prabandha* is found in Natya-Sastra written by Bharata, it can be inferred that at that time the term *Prabandha* had not come into being. By about the 6th Century the non-gandharvic forms of music established themselves rather well. Besides *Dhruvas* (stage songs), *Prabandha* the other non-gandharvic type of music emerged. This non-gandharvic type of music was called *desi* (profane or secular), while *gandharva* was called *margi* (celestial or transcendental). *Desi* music differed from region to region and readily adapted itself to popular and regional tastes.[1] It is in Brhaddesi, (6th Century), that we find a description of Prabandhas. However, Manasollasa (early 12th Century) written by Somesvara; Sangita Samayasara (late 12th Century) written by Parsvadeva and Sangita Ratnakar (13th Century) are the works wherein we find that *Prabandhas* have been dealt with elaborately. In these works there is no mention of *dhruvas*. By about the 15th Century it was on the basis of the Prabandha complex that a form of a lesser rigidity and greatly of popular appeal was gradually evolved in the shape of *Dhrupada*.

At what time after *Prabandha*, *Dhrupada* came into limelight cannot be definitely said. The historical evidence suggests that there must have been a gradual evolutionary process which resulted in the emergence of *Dhrupada* from their progenitors, the *Prabandha*.[2]

The Classical Music of India has been divided into two broad groups viz. the *Gandharva* (celestial) and the *Gana* (profane).[3] The *Gandharva* is held to have been devotional in content and its aim was presumably of a spiritual kind rather than to please the senses. In it *Svara* (the note) was in first place, the *Tala* (rhythm) in the second place and the *Pada* (text) in the third place.

---

1. Matanga Muni, Brhadesi Verse 13-14, p. 2.
2. Srivastava, Indurama, 'Dhrupada', p. 2.
3. Sangita Ratnakara of Sarangdeva, Vol. II, Chapter 4, Verse I, p. 202.

The other type of music *Gana*, although means every type of music, but mostly adapted to the taste of common mortals, with the primary purpose of pleasing the senses rather than propitiating the Gods. It could of course be devotional in content and in fact most of the times it was, but the main purpose always remained that of pleasing the senses of human beings. Thus *Gana* adapted itself to changing requirements of society and culture and was transformed in accordance with the requirements of time, place and culture. It is to this broad category of classical music that *Dhrupada* belongs.

The *Gana* has two aspects — the *Anibaddha* (unstructured) and the *Nibaddha* (structured). The *Anibaddha Gana* refers to the type of singing which is not bound by *Dhatus* and *Angas*. The *Nibaddha Gana* is bound by*Dhatus* as well as *Angas* The *Nibaddha Gana* is referred to as *Prabandha Vastu* and *Rupaka*."[1]

It is important to keep in mind that like the *Gana* the *Prabandha* also is used in two senses, a general and a specific. In its general sense it means, 'a composition' and it is in this sense that it is synonymous with *Nibaddha Gana*. In its specific or technical sense, it refers to a particular form of singing which had elements of both aspects of *Gana* - the *anibaddha* as well as the *Nibaddha*. The *anibaddha* aspect found its expression in the form of *alapati* and the *Nibaddha* or the structured aspect, found its expression in the form of the composition. The *Dhrupada* belongs to the *Gana* category of classical music and as such manifests the *anibaddha* as well as the *nibaddha* aspects of *Gana*..

Dhruvas; of Natyashastra reveal that there is no similarity of it with the *Dhrupada* form of singing. They were of five types used mainly to enhance the effect of the different situations occurring in a dramatic performance. They were of five classes e.g.

(a) *Praveshiki* (related to entrance) (b) *Aksepiki* (Related to diversion) (c) *Naiskramiki* (Related to departure) (d) *Prasadiki* (for calming down the audience) (e) *Antara* (Related to transition). The commonness of the word *dhruva* in both *dhrupada* as well as *dhruva Prabandha* indeed

1. Sharangdeva, 'Sangeet Ratnakar II, Chapter 4, Verse 6, p. 204.

tempts one to think that they ought to be same or at any rate to have a close link. Such a view however is not substantiated by facts.[1]

Dhrupadas have been evolved from *Prabandha About Prabhanda* we get examples in Manasollasa written by Somesvara II, Śangita Ratnakara (13th Century A.D.) written by Sharangadeva and Sangitaraja written by Maharana Kumbhakarna (1433-1468 A.D.). Somesvara tells us that the Prabandhas are mostly hymns in praise of Gods and goddesses like Visnu, Shankara, Brahma, Saraswati, Gauri, Mahalakshmi, Chandika and so on. There were also *Prabandhas* in laudation of human beings of great beauty, sublimity and power. *Dhrupada* seems to be related to the tradition of religious hymns which were sung in the temples, since, when *Prabandhas* gave way to *Dhrupada*, the Bhakti movement of Vallabh Sampradaya was in its full force. The main reason of Bhakti movement at that time, is associated with the book, Bhagavata Purana, written in about 900 A.D. and different schools of bhakti which arose during this time under the teachings of Nimbarka, Madhava, Visnusvamni, Vallabha and Caitanya, who worshipped Krishna as an incarnation of Vishnu. In this famous Vaishnavite temples of Nathdwara Vishnupur, Dwarika, Jagannathpuri, Mathura, Vrindavana etc. singing and playing instruments along with dancing was performed at the sun rise, sunset and during the night. This tradition survives at some temples even today. These religious songs are accompanied by *Mridang* and were called *Kirtans*. The Sanskrit *Prabandha* s given in our ancient classical writings are more or less similar to these *Kirtanas*. The Gita Govinda of Jaidev is also a collection of such Prabandhas. Around the ninth Century onwards, the Sanskrit religious songs were being substituted by the songs composed in Desi and *Prakrit* languages. In this process the famous poets of Bhakti period composed innumerable religious songs of this kind which were sung in temples. These songs were well composed and provided scope for *Alap* and *Layakari*. *Dhrupadas* in laudation of Visno and his incarnations were

---

1. Srivastava, Indurama "Dhrupada', p. 18.

called Visnupadas. During 14th and 15th Century it was usual for Vaisnavas like Chaitanya, to roam around with their *Veena* and sing *Dhrupadas* in the form of devotional songs.

Dhrupadas retained it's overwhelming preoccupation with hymns in praise of Krishna. The language of *Dhrupada* should have also been Sanskrit but no such Dhrupada has till now been reported but mostly all *Dhrupadas*, were in *Madhyadesiya*[1]

It was during this period that *Dhrupada* caught the attention of the Hindu and Muslim rulers. Main Cultural Centre of *Madhyadesa* was Gwalior and at this time Raja Dugarendra Singh (reign A.D. 1425-1459) was king of Gwalior[2]. Raja Dugarendra Singh was a great lover and patron of music. In his court the musician, Visnudasa composed several *Visnupadas*.[3] He provided the right and appropriate environment for the development of *Visnupadas* Subsequently Gwalior was ruled by Raja Kirti Singh (reign A.D. 1459-1480)[4] and Raja Kaluanamalla (reign A.D. 1480-1486)[5], and their contributions to music are not known. Raja Man Singh succeeded to the throne of Gwalior in A.d. 1486 and ruled till 1516. Raja Man Singh gave *Dhrupada* immense encouragement and introduced many refinements in it. Through these refinements he presented *Dhrupada* in a new form which was called the *Darabari Dhrupada*. On account of this contribution Raja Man Singh Tomar is known as the originator of the Dhrupada style.[6] It is further mentioned by Faqirullah that *Dhrupada* is a form composed by Raja Man Singh of Gwalior. He composed this style with the help of Nayak Bakshoo, Bhannu, Mahmood Lohang and Karna.[7] Abul Fazal has reported in Ain-I-Akbari that Raja Man Singh Tomar, the ruler of Gwalior with the assistance

---

1. Bhatakhande, Vishnu Narayan, 'Hindustani Sangita Paddhati' Part IV, p. 46.
2. Dvivedi, Gwalior Ke Tomartha, pp. 76-93.
3. Dvivedi, Madhyadesiya Bhasa, pp. 94 - 112.
4. Dvivedi, 'Gwalior Ke Tomartha', pp. 113-127.
5. Ibid.
6. Faqirullah, 'Rag Darpan', Hindi Trans. Dvivedi MAM, p. 91.
7. Ibid. p. 39.

of Nayak Bakshoo, Macchu and Bhannu, who were the most distinguished musicians of their time, introduced a popular style of melody which was approved even by the most refined taste.[1] Tohfat-ul-Hind has written that, "A poetic composition which is divided into four parts, and each part of which has a specific name, is known as *Dhrupada*. It is said that Raja Man Singh was the innovator of this type of song, but the truth is known only to the God Almighty.[2] Herbert A. Popely, Captain Willard, Sir William Jones, N. Angustus, Sir Ousley and Dr. Griffiths all consider that *Dhrupad* has its origin from the time of Raja Man Singh of Gwalior. However, present authors and musicians are of the view that these types of music prevailed in Bengal and other provinces under various names and styles, *Visnupada Dhrupada* etc., which were generally sung by the beggar-minstrels. Raja Man Singh Tomar and his companions were not the inventors of the *Dhrupada* form.[3] Faqirullah, while comparing the musicians of Man Singh's Court with those of Akbar's Court musician, has written that since Raja Man Singh was known that great musicians seldom assemble at one place for a long time, Raja Man Singh along with them wrote the book, Mankutuhal, so that it will be helpful for the coming generations and further mentions that musicians of Akbar's Court were all *atais*, while as of Man Singh's Musicians were the best and knew both theory and practical music.[4]

Presently it is generally believed that Raja Man Singh Tomar and his companions brought the older and cruder form of heterogeneous tradition to homogeneous art form by weaving into the existing popular music the woof of traditional practices, usages and ideas which, far from rendering it foolishly grandiloquent, gave it a new vigour and status. Thus the *Dhrupada* was not only to retain the twists and turns of folk types that had gone into it, but was soon to acquire the polish, embellishment and serenity of

---

1. Prajanananda Swami, 'Historical Study of Indian Music', p. 164.
2. See Tohfat-ul-Hind, Edited by N.H. Ansari.
3. Goswami O, 'The Story of Indian Music'. p. 124.
4. Faqirullah, 'Rag Darpan', Trans. Dvivedi, pp. 22-23.

the classical form undergoing many changes at the hands of many masters.[1] *Dhrupada* type of *Prabandha* took a new shape and novel course, and it was not invented, but only revived and rejuvenated by Raja Man Singh, who, assisted by Hindu and Muslim musicians of outstanding merit, estabished a Gwalior School of Music.[2]

After the death of Raja Man Singh his son, Raja Vikramaditya also known as Vikramajita (Reign A.D. 1516-1523) ascended the throne. He was defeated by Ibrahim Lodi and died in Panipat while fighting with Babar along with Ibrahim Lodi. During this period the school of music of Gwalior broke up and large number of musicians of Gwalior court had to find other patrons. Musicians who were devotees of Krishna went to *Mathura* and others to *Vridavana* while others found patronage in the courts of others kings. This dispersion spread and popularised the *Dhrupada* style. During the period of sixteenth Century till around the middle of eighteenth Century, *Dhrupada* was the most popular form of Indian Classical Music. It was during the period of Muhammad shah Rangile (reign A.D. 1719-1748), that newer styles of music like *Khayala, Thumri, Tappa etc.* had become more popular than the *dhrupada* style and Mohammad Shah was more fond of these newer styles. *Dhrupada* was being thrown into the background.

The distinctive quality of *dhrupada* lies in the beauty and the elegance with which it uses the *svaras* The raga is rendered here in its purest form. No mixing of other ragas is permitted in *Dhrupada* as the case with the other more recent styles like *Khayala, Thumri*, *Tappa* etc. The expression of raga and the significance of the mode is conveyed at its most profound level. The other quality of *dhrupada* is its *Tala* or rhythm. A *dhrupada* singer is required to have perfect control over the *Tala*. In earlier times there were *Dhrupada* songs in which a singer had to follow a different *Tala* each time. The first line for instance may be in *Cautala* contained in twelve *matras* while the very next line may well be in *Jhaptala* which

1. Goswami O, The story of India Music p. 124.
2. Prajanananda Swami, ' A Historical Study of India Music', pp.164-165.

contains ten *matras*. The other quality of the *Dhrupada* is the poetic or literary content. The text of *Dhrupada* is distinguished by the sublimity of its meaning. This is perhaps the only musical form where the poetic qualities are held to be just as important as the melody. Thus *Dhrupada* represents a unique balance of *Svara, Tana* and *Pada.*

In Dhrupada, raga is presented in its clearest and purest form. Alapa is the first step in singing of Dhrupada and only *Tanapura* or *Tambura* is used as an accompaniment. The singer demonstrates the important notes of raga as well as insignificant ones. The raga has no text but in earlier times it was customary to sing *alap* with phrases like *Om Ananta Narayana Hari or Tun Hi Ananta hari* as a kind of invocation of God. Later on these phrases disappeared but left *nom tom* as a vestige.[1] The alap is performed in four steps. In the first step the notes of lower register are sung and in later steps the notes of progressively higher registers are sung. It is followed by singing of composition without any interruption and a beat is provided by the drumer. The composition is of four[2] or five melodic components which are verses and are known as *Dhatus* viz. *Sthayi, antara, sanchari* and *abhoga*. In earlier times, *dhrupada* had only three *dhatus* viz. *Udgraha, antara* or *dhruva* and *Bhoga.* In late 18th Century *Udgraha dhatu* was replaced by *Sthayi.* The *Sthayi* means constant, fixed or basic. In singing the *dhrupada* composition the singer after completing each *dhatu* returns once again to the *Sthayi* which forms a base of *dhatu.*

The second component is called *antara* which means different. it is generally sung in the notes of the upper part of the upper register.

The *dhatu* of *dhrupada* is sanchari which means flowing or freely moving, which probably was developed towards the end of 19th Century. Prior to this time the third part of *Dhrupada* was called *abhoga*. Since this *dhatu* used to be long, it was split into two portions, the first portion called as *sanchari* and second being known as *abhoga* Here the

1. Puchwale, Rajabhaiya, 'Dhrupada Dhamar Gayana', Ramacandra Sangita Pustak Bhandar, Gwalior, 1954, p. 2.
2. Srivastava.Indurama - Dhrupada, p. 48.

singer has the liberty to sing in any register and can easily move from lower to higher register.

The fourth *dhatu* is *abhoga* which means completion. This piece contains the name of composer or his patron and this too can be sung in any register. The *laya* in *Dhrupada* is characterised by the fact that during the same performance it changes a number of times. Each acceleration is in multiples of two, three, four, 1.5, 1.25 or 7/6 and so on of the basic tempo which is called *thaha*. Since the *tala* is fixed, accelerating the tempo implies that with each acceleration, the singer has to compress more and more syllables either in *alap* or during singing of composition in a *matra*. Each change in *laya* produces a sort of an electrifying effect on the audience. The capacity to very the tempo at will in precise multiples, demands, on the part of the performer, a perfect control of his delivery and a very precise sense of the beat. A performer who could demonstrate this in ample measures and in perfect precision, easily and justifiably earned the admiration of his audience. The good *Dhrupada* singer demonstrates even the most complicated *layakaris*. Most *Dhrupada* singers presently are quite content and they can demonstrate a few of the simpler *layakaris* like *Duguna, tinguna* and *cauguna*. The singer begins his *alap* in *thaha* which is basic and slowest *laya*, and is called *Vilambit laya*. Step by step the singer, while still in alap, moves to faster and faster *layas*. The farthest range of *Laya* reached by the singer is called *druta laya* as and *laya* in between *thaha* and *druta laya* is known as *madya laya*. Having reached the fastest *laya* the singer returns to the *thaha* on which ends the *alapa*.

Another art that the *dhrupada* singer demonstrates is called *bolabanta* which is the art of singing piece by piece, small phrases of the text in different tonal combinations and in different *layas*. In this an immense charm and variety is brought in the singing.

Another component of *dhrupada* is *tala*. It forms the basis of all Indian vocal, Instrumental Music and Dance. Each cycle of *tala* being known as *avarta* and beginning of *avarta* is called *sama*. In most of the *dhrupadas tala* has been mentioned, but those *talas* have now been forgotten. The modern *dhrupada* singers sing in *talas* which are prevalent these days.

The *Dhrupada* came to develop certain distinct melodic styles which are known as *banis*. There are five kinds of *banis* which are *Suddha Bani*, *Goudhar Bani*, *Dagar Bani*, *Khandar Bani* and *Naohar Bani*. According to some scholars the *Bani's* are related to the five *Svarashrita Geetis*. *Goudhar Bani* resembles the Shastrik *Suddha Geeti*. Dhrupada of the *Goudhar Bani*, according to the teachings of Mian Tansen, are sung in a pure and melodious way containing *meends* in straight lines according to the structure of the *Ragas* Mian Tansen himself was a master of this style, although he was proficient in other styles as well and in the line of his youngest son, Bilas Khan, this style was mainly used.

Dagar Bani :-Dagar Bani resembles the *Vinna Geeti*. It contains *'meends'* in curved lines with sweet and subtle *Gamakas* or vibrations. *Dagar Bani* is a very charming exposition of *Dhrupada* music which was used by the disciples of Swami Haridasa and also by Saraswati Devi, the daughter of Mian Tansen and her husband Misri Singh.

Khandar Bani resembles *Besora Geeti* as it contains quick *Gamakas* This style was used in vocal Music by Baj Bhadur and also by Misri Singh in his songs and Veena recitals. Later on, the descendants of Misri Singh used both *Dagar Vani* and *Khandar Bani*.

Naohar Bani :- Naohar Bani resembles to some extent to *Goudi Geeti*. It contains *chhut Alankar*, that is the jumpy notes with the *Gamakas* This *Bani* always used as a part of the Dhrupada of some other *Bani*. It is said that Sri Chand, a disciple of Swami Haridasa, was a master of this style. [1]

According to Karam Imam[2], *banis* derived their names from the places where they developed and flourished. Accordingly *Goudhar Bani* was introduced by Tansen and was started in Gwalior, the dialect of which was known as *Gobarahara*. *Khnadar Bani* said to have been introduced by Samokhan Singh, originated in Khandara Pradesh, the

1. Roy Chaudhuri Birendra Kishore, 'Indian Music and Mian Tansen'. pp. 7-8.
2. Acharya Brahaspati, 'Dhrupadas Aur Hindi Sahitya', pp. 276 - 277.

dialect of which is known as a *Khandari* The *Dagar Bani* which is said to have been introduced by Brija Chanda, originated in Dagar, which was near Delhi and which is known now-a-days as Danga.[1] The *Naohar Bani*, which is said to have been introduced by Srichanda originated in a place called Nauha.

The *Banis* of the songs indicated the words which were used in accordance with emotions or *'Rasas'* contained in the *Ragas* and with their appropriate styles in the music. Thus the words, emotions, ragas and styles of music were chosen to fit one another. In the *dhrupada* of the *Goudhar Bani* those ragas were chosen which expressed the emotion of peace and calmness, that is *Shanta Rasa* In the *Dagar Bani* the poems and the Ragas expressd either sweetness or pathos that is *'Madhura Rasa'* and *'Karuna Rasa'*. The *Khandar Bani* expressed the heroic spirit and valour that is *'Vir Rasa'* and *Naohar Bani* containing surprising movements of the notes expressed *'Adbhut Rasa'*. The Ragas chosen for these *Banis* expressed the emotions suitable for them. But this uniformity of the *Banis* or words, the *Ragas*, the *rasas* and the style was not particularly observed, sometimes after the golden age of *Mian Tansen* and the *Darbar* of Akbar the Great.[2]

Each *Gharana* of *Dhrupada* specialised in one of these four *Banis* but also adopted other banis in their musical demonstrations. In eighteenth and nineteenth Century three main *Senia Gharanas* were formed which were, *Senia Gharana* of Jaipur specialising in the *Dhrupada* of the *Dagar Vani* The line of the Bilas Khan specialised in the *Dhrupada* of *Goudhar Bani* although they also took up the *Dagar Bani* to some extent. The *Senia* musicians of the time of Misri Singh were specialists of the *Dagar and Khandar Bani*. Among other *Gharanas* of *Dhrupadas* which grew up with the teachings of the Senia musicians or of the disciples of Haridasa Swami, the musicians of *Betia* based their *Dhrupadas* on the *Khandar Bani* and the famous musicians of Bishnupur made *Gaudhar Bani* the basis of their music.

---

1. Acharya Brahaspati, 'Dhrupadas Aur Hindi Sahitya', p. 277.
2. Roy Chaudhuri, Birendra Kishore, 'Indian Music and Mian Tansen', p. 8.

The Vocalists of Mathura, mainly sang *Dhrupadas* of *Dagar Bani*. Another famous *gharana* of Dhrupada led by Ustad Bahram Khan, flourished in Rajasthan. This *gharana* is now called *Dagar Gharana*. The vocalists of this *Gharana*, however, have combined the *Dagar* and the *Khandar Bani*, in the execution of their songs. all these musicians used *Naohar Bani* in a variation.[1]

The *Banis* had a short life span. In the course of time the different *banis* merged with each other and lost most of their distinctive qualities. As a result, when a *Dhrupada* singer of today performs, it is difficult to say which of the various *Banis* he is combining in his particular performance. However, since the *Suddha* and *Dagar Bani* were less ornamented and offered a better scope for *Layakaris* these are the ones which are predominantly reflected in the performance of a modern singer.[2] According to Dr. Sumati Mutatkar, Agra *Gharana*, which originally was a *Dhrupada Gharana* represented the *Naohar Bani*ni[3]. The Jaipur *Gharana* of Ustad Alladiya Khan, according to his own statement, represented the *Dagar Bani* The beginning of *Dhrupada* is presently believed to be in 13th & 14th Century A.D. and reached its zenith of popularity during the 16th /17th and 18th Century A.D. when most of the renowned musicians of that time were accomplished *Dhrupada* singers. It is believed that Tansen became an exponent of the *Dhrupad* style and by his high creativity and genius, he raised the status of *Dhrupad* as the highest expression of music.

Dhrupad was in traditional type. Raja Man Singh Tomar and Tansen turned it into a new shape, yet retaining the elements of its older tradition. The *Dhrupad* outgrew its early form and boldly ventured into unexplored regions, acquiring a new status. Goswami Ji says, "It acquired a newness with the magic touch of Tansen for it had an inherent strength and capacity to absorb elements of alien origin without succumbing to them".

---

1. Ibid., pp. 9-10.
2. Srivastava Indurama 'Dhrupada', p. 51.
3. Personal Communication with Dr. Sumati Mutatkar.

By his genius, Tansen brought a rare beauty, elasticity and dignity to *Dhrupada* Tansen based all his musical creations on the *Dhrupada Padhati*, while assimilating some beautiful forms of the Persian music.[1] He enriched the Dhrupada style with some Persian ornamentations.[2] Tansen reached the fountains of the *Ragas* which are the embodiments of the cosmic melodies, and he gave the most profound and richest expressions of *Raga* nelodies through the system of the Hindustani *Dhrupada*[3]. Tansen reshaped the entire Dhrupada music by the addition of new ornamentations in*Meend, Gamaka etc.*. which were lacking in them[4]. Swami Prajanananda states, "Mian Tansen and other eminent musicians gained abiding fame for the culture of *Dhrupada*".[5] *Dhrupad* became the most prominent feature of music culture of that time i.e. in the 16th and 17th Century.

Tansen's genius of course found its expression predominantly in music, but as a poet also his contributions have eternal worth. Although the exact modes of his songs are not easy to discover and are confined to the *Gharanas* of his descendants and disciples, but the compositions are still there and we can easily determine their poetical values which are sublime indeed. The songs of Tansen have been devoted to his spiritual realisation. The essence of the Vedantic teachings is the basis of the realisation of the great master like Tansen.

We find also many outstanding songs composed by him in praise of the kings and the emperors. These songs contain remarkable synthesis of the Vedanta, the *Bhakti Sastra* and the mysticism of the *Sufi* cult t.[6]

This *Dhrupada* of Tansen is in laudation of King Akbar (1556-1605).

---

1. Goswami O, " The Story of Indian Music", p. 124.
2. Roy Chaudhuri Birendra Kishore, Indian Music and Mian Tansen', p. 26.
3. Ibid.
4. Ibid. p. 25.
5. Ibid, p. 26.
6. Roy Chaudhuri Birendra Kishore, 'Indian Music and Mian Tansen', p .18.

शुभ नरवत तरवत बैठो राजत छाजत
सब मूलक खलक जै बिघना किए सब
छत्र धरे ते सब लागे सबु सेवा करन
धन धन चक्रवती नरेश अकबर दुखहरन तानसैन
ऐसो सूरपुरी नर नरेन्द्र नरन ।

Its meaning is that *Cakravarti* King Akbar adorned the throne at a time when there were many auspicions planets all round. Even the wicked people started serving the king by holding his Umbrella. His Kingdom is like a noblemen and kings alive. The king removes all the suffering of the people. Tansen, the composer blesses the king for having such fortune.

There are many songs of devotion to the supreme divine and also to the Gods.

An invocation to Krishna, the benevolent god who brings comfort and takes away the suffering of everyone, has been made in the following *Dhrupada*

मोहन सृष्टि के आधर तन को
अब राख लीजै गोपाल
नैन प्राण सुख दीजे तन तैं
दुख दूर कीज्ये इतनी विनती
मेरी सुन लीजे हाल
पतित पावन करूणा सिन्धु
दीन दुख भंजन अनेक रूप
लीलाधरी भक्त बछल जुग जुग भए कृपाल
मदन मोहन मधुसूदन मुरार गज
सुदामा द्रोपदी सहाय करि
तानसेन प्रभु भक्त प्रतिपाल ।

Meaning : O Mohana, you are supporter and the protector of the universe; please protect this body. Kindly give solace to my eyes and my soul; take away the suffering of the body. Please answer my supplication. You are the resurrector of the fallen ones. You are an ocean of pity. You are the remover of suffering of the helpless. You have myraid forms and you play your part in innumerable ways. You are kind and loving to your devotees. You are Madhusūdana. You are Murāri. You came to the rescue of Gaja (Elephant), Sudama and Draupadi. Tansen says, O Lord, you are the nurturer of your devotees.

There are many Dhrupadas of Tansen which have already been described at the end of IInd Chapter.

CONTRIBUTION OF SENIAS' IN DHRUPADA AND THEIR COMPOSITIONS

From the period of Tansen upto the beginning of present Century the descendants of Tansen, who were called Seni Musicians, were regarded as authorities on Hindustani Classical Music.

His sons, Tan-Tarang Khan and Bilas Khan, both became the pioneers of *Dhrupada* style. Faqirullah says that Tan-Tarang Sen got the rank of *Gandharva*[1] They both developed the *Dhrupada* form of music with certain distinct melodies. They used to sing *Dhrupada* in a *Shuddha Bani*. *Rag* Bilas Khani Todi was invented by Bilas Khan which is very popular these days. There are many *Dhrupada*s. Only a few of them are available. Here is the *Dhrupada* of Tan-Tarang describing Krishna Leela. Music is also evident in them. He is known as true their of his father Tansen. His compositions are mature in *Dhrupada* characteristics. His language is simple and has flow. He is adept in depicting the picture of what he wants to describe. In the following one he describes the beauty of a woman drawing water in which the *Alankars* have been set in natural way.

---

1. Faqirullah, 'Rag Darpan', p. 130

चुनरी आरी त्यारी पंचरंग पैहरे सु पनीश्रा
गगरीआं भरें आवत और दोऊ हाथ ग्रीवानि धरें
गौरे भुंजनि में गाढें वंश फुनि दड़वानि में स्याम चुरी
हथेरिनि नौहिनी मेंहदी गेहेरोई रंग करें
उसासति वेसरि दधिसुत डोलत ता मध मुष प्रसिधि
भोंहे तानें अधर दसन दंपति सों कांननि वीरे गरें मोतनि लरें
कुछ उत्तंग मतंग से दैर्शअत वनीता जनौरी सु चौबे कुलल भरें
जै हरि जोति सूरज सों होड़ वरी आगे बिछीआ
बाजनें तिनि मध लाल गुघाऊें लागऊ महावर पत्रनि तरें
तानतरंग प्रभु को मन मोहन गति से दिषावत
सो मुसकाई वाल हरें [1]

In the next *Dhrupada* Tan-Tarang says, that a *Gwalin* (Cowmaid), though sarcastically or ironically rebukes Lord Krishna that he begs of every lay person, but in the heart of her hearts, she rejoices the teasings from him. The language is simple, pleasing and idiomatic. This *Dhrupada* shows that the woman felt happy though she pretended to have disliked it.

सुंघेई मांगि लैहो दांन
हम पर जाति को रहो न नातौ
मन मिलि बातें काहें को बनावत राषौ जू अपनौ ग्यान
जैसी छल बल की बतीआ काहें को करत हों जू
जैसी न देशी सुनी कहूं कान
तान तरंग प्रभु अपने ही गो की करत
मानत न काहूं की आन [2]

Bilas Khan, the youngest son of Tansen, was a good

---

1. Acharya Brahaspati, 'Dhrupad Aur Uska Vikas', p. 296.
2. 'Rag Mala', p. 76.

Dhrupada Singer. His *Dhrupadas* described Krishna *Leela* The music in his *Dhrupadas* was good. In the following *Dhrupada* he describes the beauty of a beloved (*Nayaka*) and hero her lover, appreciate the same. The language is simple and pleasing and has good appeal.

पिय के मन में न नैनन भावें तेरो जोबन नियको
तेरे रूप रस बस भयो प्रानपति तौ जिय चाहे,
आन न काहु तियको;
रूप जौबन तो है दीनों करतार बनाय
आली कौप ना रहौ गर्व हिय को
प्रभु बिलास नवललाल रिसाल प्रीत नई
आली री आनन्द बड़ो जिय को [1]

In the following *Dhrupada*, Bilas Khan advises people to learn music from Tansen. In it he feels that those who want to make music a means of liv•lihood, though they may be otherwise good in all respects, should take lessons from Tansen. The language is good and may make the advice acceptable to those for whom it is meant.

कौन भ्रम भूल्यौ रे मन अज्ञानी
सीखत न राग रंग तान अक्षर सुधबानी
और स्वारथ सों अनम गंवायो
विद्या बात अधिक सयानी
जै साधु गुणी भए तिन कौन गुण की मत ठानी
बिलास के प्रभु को जो भलो चाहत
तो मिलाओ तानसेन गुरू ज्ञानी [2]

---

1. Krsnananda Vyas, Rag Kalpadrum, Vol. I, p. 121.
2. Ibid., p. 129.

Another *Dhrupada* singer was Lal Khan, the son-in-law of Bilas Khan. His style of singing resembled Tansen's singing, which he acquired from Tansen as well as Bilas Khan. He was unparalleled in *Dhrupada* singing.

Khushal Khan, who was the son of Lal Khan, was a best *Dhrupada* singer in Shah Jehan's Court. Being a favourite singer of Shah Jehan, he used to include his name in his compositions.

Khushal Khan's and Bisram Khan's *Dhrupadas* in Rag *Todi* were so much liked by Shah Jehan that he used to get totally absorbed and intoxicated. Murshid Quli Khan's order to accompany Aurangzeb to South was signed by emperor Shah Jehan under the influence of the music of Khushal Khan and Bisram Khan.

DHRUPADAS OF KHUSHAL KHAN

During Aurangzeb's time *Dhrupada* was popular to the same degree of admiration, as is evident from the following *Dhrupada* song which has been composed by Khushal Khan in praise of the emperor.

आयो आयो रे महाबलि आलमगीर
जाकी धाक देखे कोऊ धरे न धीर
अपबली तपबली आलीजंग और तेऊ भाटल गंभीर
दक्षिण दलमले विकल गढ़ हलहले
जाकौ तौ घुआई फिरे दरियातीर
चकतावंश सुलितान औरंगज़ेब
साहिनी में साहि औलिया जिन्दावीर [1]

It has been usually found that Tansen and his descendants included the name of their patrons in their compositions (*Dhrupadas*) Here is a *Dhrupadas* composed by Khushal Khan in which he has included the name of Emperor Shah Jehan :

---

1. Ahmad Najma Parveen, 'Hindustani Music', p. 104.

बैठी री कर पै कपोल धरे रीजायें दुचिती
अनमनी आज पिया सों कछु अनबनी
रूठी सी रूठी से आननि विलषी सी मनु मारें तानस कीयें
मानत न काऊ को कहो सकल त्रीअनी में तूही मन मानी
शाहिजहां पीअ तेरे रस बस भए नै बना तू बनी ।

Next *Dhrupadas* ; composed by Khushal Khan in which is included the name of Aurangzeb. Brahaspati Ji says that Khushal Khan was for Thirteen years in the court of Aurangzeb reign (1659-1707).

तै तौ आपु ही में बनाई अनूपम चौपरि ऐ
रूप जोबन गुण वानिक बिसति माघ वसीकरण
घर कीनौ फुनि दीनों त्रविधि कटाछि पासे करि
वौ सुम दांव वतन तौही कौं फुरेरि औरनि के
चौक चाक बांधि बांधि चतुर बतीआं कीनी जाही तै पूजी सार
सौतिनि सों बाजू पीअ जीति लीनी
साहि औरंगजेब रीझि रूचि सौं कंठ लगाई भुज भर [1]

Niyamat Khan (Sadarang) who was a top *Dhrupada* singer from the beginning of 18th Century till middle of 18th Century was supposed to be God's great gift in Northern India. He had a magic in his voice and used to compose Dhrupadas with great maturity, freshness and colourfulness. In the following composition he depicts the feelings of a recently married woman who tries to play tricks with her bridegroom but does not know the technique and tries not to incur displeasure of her lover in any way. Such a description of her feelings in simple and good language is a rare speciality of Niyamat Khan (Sadarang).

कौऊ तौ मौहि बताऔ री पीअ सों मान करिवें की दवा
पै ऐंसैं कीजै जामें नैक मलीन न हौवे और अपनी हूं बात रहौ
सब

1. 'Raag Mala', p. 65.

उनिकि कहा कहौं वे तौ निपट प्रवीन रसिक लाल,
दैखि रहे अनैग जोविनि की फरकनि तिनि सो छिपि सकै कब
यह भूल मो मन आई गई तातें सदारंग पीअ सों
रिस हूं मैं रुसीजें कैबहूं अब जब तब [1]

In the following *Dhrupada* Niyamat Khan (Sadarang), points in words the feelings of a bride separated for long from her lover, when the Coel in spring sings melodious songs and rouses the feelings of the lady. In the intensity of feelings in separation increased by the song of the bird, she entreats the bird to spare her from the pain its song causes to her. In this composition Sadarang has shown that he can dive very deep into the psyche of human beings.

अब तो कोकिल धूम मचाई पीआ विदेस
मोहि पाह अकेली विरहनी जानि सताई
एक तौं हती मैं वैरिनि उनकी करत चवाओन आई
बोलि बोलि जब बान से मारत तन मन बैघत जाई
कुकि कुकि डरपाई री जीअ में आति ही अक बड़ाई
चीतौ वसन्त जब आयौ फागुन
अब कहा करौ मोरी गाई
ये समये सुधि लीजौ सदारंग सुषदाई दुषदाइ [2]

Feroz Khan (Adarang) was the son-in-law and nephew of Niyamat Khan (Sadarang). He was trained in the same way as Niyamat Khan. He was very good *Dhrupada* singer of his time. He has said that when a man gets a chance to sing, he should start singing by taking the name of Sadarang first.

In the following *Dhrupada* it is described how a woman,

---

1. Krsnananda Vyas, 'Raag Kalpadrum' , Vol. I, p. 119.
2. Collection of Late Gopal Singh Ji, Pakhawaj Player of Gwalior Gharana.

passionately loving her lover, would not hesitate to go out of way to satisfy herself. She is inviting her associates to accompany her shedding all apprehensions of social restraints. In it is apparent that Adarang could well asses and gauge the workings of the mind of a woman to meet her lover. The language used is appropriate and musical.

ए री यह औसर भली है अलबेली चतुर नारी
चलि चलि पीअ पास
नव सत सिंगार साज तजि दौंअ लाज आस
अधराति भई चन्द्र हू चढ़ौ अकास
मेरीअै कहौ मांनि अैंसी छाड़ि कै रसरी काम तुम
अब जोनि करि विविधि विलास आस
जब ते निहारो तोहि अदारंग जब तै महोमद
सा प्यारे - देषि प्राण लागि रही तैरी बास [1]

Adrang's next *Dhrupada* is concerns the Holi Festival.

अरगजा गुलाल ले कैसरि रंग पिचकारी भरि भरि छोड़त
अतर गुलाब ओर चौवा चन्दन पीअ मुष
मीजत बनि बनि
वनिता सौ तब वेहू लाल मिलि गए
गुपित गांठ तक टोरत
लाज सकुच छाड़ि दीनी लैगनि की जब ऐक ऐक
को जो बस करि रस में बौरत
कहा कहौ समयौ अति सुन्दर सदारंगीले ऐ नोंला
सी तिनिको भुज भेंटत कुचहि मरोरत
मध कों मतवारो अदारंग करि दौर गरव हीवा
डारत मसकारेत

1. Rag Kalpadrum, p. 127.

ऐ सखी री या वौहति दिननि को विछुरौ मिलौ
याते फागु प्रीति वाहन जुरत [1]

Mahavat Khan or Manrang was son of Niyamat Khan. He had written many Dhrupadas and *Hori's* n honour of his father and in honour of Muhammad Shah Rangile. His Dhrupada compositions are giving at the end of this chapter.

Charju Khan, and Jeewan Khan, were the sons of Manrang, and were the masters of *Dhrupada* singing.

Jafar Khan, Pyar Khan and Basat Khan were the three sons of Charju Khan. All the three brothers were of great reputation in playing *Been* as well as singing *Dhrupada*. Charju Khan had one daughter through whom Bahadur Hussain Khan was born. Pyar Khan adopted Bahadur Hussain Khan and trained him in *Dhrupada* as well as in Insturmental Music. He along with Amir Khan, his son-in-law were founders of Rampur Gharana. They both were masters in *Dhrupada* as well as in Instrumental Music. At the end of this Chapter, Bahadur Hussain Khan's *Sargam* in *Rag Iman Kalyan & Goud Sarang* , is given.

Haider Khan and Bahadur Khan were sons of Jeewan Khan. They were both Ustads in *Dhrupada* as well as in Instrumental Music.

Turap Ali Khan, Umrao Khan and Muhammad Ali Khan were all sons of Haider Khan. Although they were great instrumentalists, yet they all were masters in *Dhrupada* also.

Ali Muhammad, Muhammad Ali and Reyast Ali were all sons of Basat Khan. Ali Muhammad Khan, the eldest son of Basat Khan, was appointed by the Raja of Varanasi as the Chief Musician of his Court. He had profound knowledge of *Ragas* and could develop any *Raga* for hours. Muhammad Ali Khan was a good Dhrupad singer and an accomplished *Been* and *Sur-Sringar* Player.

His compositions are given at the end of this Chapter. Ali Muhammad Khan imparted lessons on Vocal Music of *Dhrupad* and Instrumental Music on Been and *Sur-Sringar* to Wazir Khan of Rampur. Wazir Khan became the

---

1. Acharya Brahspati, 'Dhrupad Aur Uska Vikas' p. 309.

master of *Dhrupada* and instrumental music also. His compositions are also given at the end of this chapter,.

Kazam Ali, Sadiq Ali and Nisar Ali were sons of Jafar Khan. Sadiq Ali and Nisar Ali became attached to the Court of the Raja of Varanasi. The Raja had great respect for them. They excelled in *Been* also. They had many disciples in *Dhrupada* and also in Instrumental Music.

Amir Khan and Rahim Khan both were sons of Umrao Khan. Amir Khan was the son-in-law of Bahadur Hussain Khan. The Rampur *Gharana* was founded by Bahadur Hussain Khan and Amir Khan. Rahim Khan and Amir Khan had a melodius voice and were instrumentalists. Their more concentration was on Vocal Music. They always used to sing *Dhrupada* in the *Darbar*. They both were the Court Musician of Nawab Wazid Ali Shah.

Wazir Khan the son of Amir Khan. He was a melodius vocalist. He was master in *Dhrupada* and was an instrumentalist. His compositions are given at the end of this Chapter. Nazir Khan and Sagir Khan were *Dhrupada* singers, as well as instrumentalists.

Chamman Khan, Dabir Khan and Dildar Khan were sons of Nazir Khan. Dabir Khan, was one of the top and the last musicians of *Dhrupada* as well as an instrumentalist in *Senia Gharana*. He built the musical career of many musicians.

In Rampur state, Nawab Chamman Saheb, son of Nawab Haider Ali Khan, was an accomplished *Dhrupada* singer. He was the Guru and the friend of Pandit Vishnu Narayan Bhatkhande. There are many compositions of Nawab Chamman Saheb. Some of them are given at the end of this Chapter.

सेनिया घराना कृत सरगम

बिलासखानी तौड़ी [1]

स्थायी

ग	रे	ग	सा	रे	नि	सा	रे	ग	रे	ग	म	ग	रे	रे	सा
0				3								2			
सा		रे	नि़	ध	ध	म	-	नि	ध	रे	सा	रे	नि़	सा	रे
0				3								2			

अन्तरा

म	ध	सां	–	रें	नि़	सां	रें	गं	सां	रें	नि	ध	ध	ग	म
0				3								3			
नि	नि	ध	म	ग	रे	ग	म	ग	रे	रे	सा	रे	नि़	ध	ध
0				3								2			
ग	रे	ग	सा	रे	नि़	सा	रे								
0				3											

---

1. मारिफ़ुन्नग़मात, प्रथम भाग, पृष्ठ 229 ।

बहादुर हुसैन खां कृत सरगम -
राग गौडसारंग (एकताल) [1]

स्थायी

9	10	11	12	1	2	3	4	5	6	7	8
नि	सा	ग	रे	म	ग	मे	प	घ	प	म	ग
रे	ग	-	रे	सा	ऩि	घ़	—	मे	प़	ऩि	सा
ग	रे	ग	म	घ	प	म	ग	रे	ग	ग	रे
नि	सा	ग	रे								

अन्तरा

				प	मे	प	सां	-	रे	सां	-
गं	गं	रें	सां	नि	सां	गं	मं	धं	पं	मं	गं
रें	सां	नि	ध	मे	प	ध	ग	-	म	प	सां
-	रें	सां	नि	ध	प	म	ग	रे	ग	ग	रे
ऩि	सा	ग	रे								

---

1. सगीत चिंतामणि, द्वितीय खण्ड, पृष्ठ 464 ।

वजीर खां कृत सरगम

राग भैरवी, तीन ताल [1]

स्थायी

नि	स	ग	म	ध	प	ध	म	प	ग	-	म	ध	नि	सां	-
रे	सां	नि	ध	गं	रें	सां	नि	ध	नि	सां	गम	निध	पम	गरे	सा
0				3								2			

अन्तरा

ग	म	ध	नि	सां	-	रें	सां	गं	रें	सं	मं	गं	रें	सां	-
ध	नि	गं	-	नि	ध	-	ग	म	ग	रे	सा	निध	पम	गरे	सा
0				3								2			

---

1. आचार्य बृहस्पति, संगीत चिन्तामणि, पृष्ठ 581 ।

Dhrupada
Composed by Wazir Khan Raga "Ghandhari"[1]

स्थायी

कहियो उधो तुम ज्यों नेह बीज जो गवन
कीनों माधो बिरवा लागो राधा के मन ।

अन्तरा

दृगतारे कूप कीने अंसुवन जल भार भरे
पलकन सींच सींच याते और बिरवा भयो सघन वन ।।

संचारी

भूमि हरि भीर रोम रूख बन रहे पांच बेल
काम के चढ़ी जिया तन ।

आभोग

कुच काछी रखवारे फूलखल होने
लागे आयके जो देखिए जु जीवन धन ।।

---

1. Bhatkhande Vishnu Narayan, 'Sangeet Shastra,' Vol. IV, p. 488.

Dhrupada
Composed by Nawab Chhaman Sahab Raga "Bihag" (Choutal)[1]

जो लौं हि भारतण्ड चन्द्र सोहे असमान मांहि
जो लौं शेष सीस भू अचल बनी रहे
जो लौं गंगा जमुना की धार धारा मण्डल में
जो लौं कैलास में कुबेर सौ धनी रहे
जो लौं क्षीरसागर उजागर जहां बीज
जो लौं विष्णु चक्र असुरन पर गनी रहे
सादत के प्रभु रसिक श्री नवाब बहादुर जू
तो लौं जग रावरी सुकीरति बनी रहे

स्थाई

–	म	–	ग	–	सा	नी	–	प	नी	सा	सा
S	जो	S	लौं	S	हि	भा	S	र	तं	S	ड
		3		4				0		2	
स	–	स	ग	–	म॑	प	ग	म	ग	सा	सा
चं	S	द्र	स	S	हे	अ	स	S	मा	S	न
		3		4				0		2	
सा	–	स	ग	–	म॑	प	–	सा	नी	–	प
मां	S	हि	जो	S	लौं	शे	S	ष	सी	S	स
		3		4				0		2	
प	मैप	प	ग	–	म॑	प	ग	म	ग	सा	सा
भू	S	अ	च	S	ल	ब	नी	S	र	S	हे

1. Nawab Ali Khan, "Mariphoonagmat", Vol. II. p. 70.

अन्तरा

प	–	प	नी	–	नी	सां	सां		सां	–	सां
जो	S	लौं	गं	S	गा	ज	मु	S	ना	S	की
		0		2		0		3		4	
सां	–	गं	सं	नी	प	प	सां	सां	नी	–	प
धा	S	र	धा	रा	S	मं	S	ड	ल	S	मे
		0		2		0		3		4	
ग	–	गम	प	नी	नी	सां	–	गं	सां	नी	प
जो	S	S	लौं	S	कै	ला	S	स	में	S	कु
		0		2		0		3		4	
प	–	प	ग	–	मं	प	मे	म	ग	सा	सा
बे	S	र	सो	S	S	ध	नी	S	र	S	हे
		0		2		0		3		4	

संचारी

सां	–	सं	प	–	प	प	–	–	प	–	प
जो	S	लौं	छी	S	र	सा	S	S	ग	S	र
		0		2		0		3		4	
नी	नी	घ	प	–	प	सं	नी	–	नी	प	प
उ	जा	S	ग	S	र	ज	हां	S	बी	S	च
		0		2		0		3		4	
प	–	प	म॑	ग	म	प	–	गम	ग	सा	सा
जों	S	S	लौं	S	S	वि	S	षगु	च	S	कु
		0		2		0		3		4	
प	प	नी	नी	सां	सां	प	ग	म	ग	सा	सा
अ	सु	र	न	प	र	ग	नी	S	र	S	हे
		0		2		0		3		4	

आभोग

प	-	सां	सां	सां	–	सां	सां	-	सां	सां	सां
सा		द	त	से	S	प्र	भु	उ	र	सि	क
सा	-	सा	नि	-	प	प	सां	-	नी	-	प
श्री	S	न	वा	S	ब	ब	हा	S	दु	S	र
म	ग	र्म	प	-	सां	पं	गं	मं	गं	सां	सां
जू	S	तो	लों	S	ज	ग	रा	S	व	S	री
X		0		2		0		3		4	
सां	सां	-	नी	प	गम	प	ग	म	ग	सा	सा
सु	की	S	र	S	ति	ब	नी	S	र	S	हे
		0		2		0		3		4	

CHAPTER V

BEEN : (VEENA OR VINA) ITS EVOLUTION AND THE CONTRIBUTION TO IT BY SENIA'S

The word *Veena* seems to have been first used in the *Vedas.*[1] The stringed instruments known as Tata seem to have come first than the *Bitata* (stringed instruments played with bow); next came the wind instruments followed by the *metalled* ones as per our texts. A stringed instrument of *Veena* type along with other specimen instruments have been found in Mohenjodaro and Harappa ruins. It proves that *Veena* was used even before the Aryan People came to India.[2]

From this pre-historic period to the period of *Vedas* and *Samhitas*, we find both the *Veena* and the *Mridanga* mentioned. In the *Asvamedha* sacrifice they used *Veena* as an accompaniment to chant and the *Veda* extols it as : Thus, the *Veena*, is verily the embodiment of beauty and prosperity.[3] A *Veena Vadak* or a lute player, is included in the list of victims of *Purusamedha Yagna* (Human sacrifice) *in the* Yajur Veda and elsewhere.[4]

In *Vedic* period *Veena* had been used as a

1. Deva B.C., 'Musical Instruments', p 79.
2. Goswami O, 'The Story of Indian Music', pp. 292-293.
3. Ibid, p. 79.
4. Vedic Index, Vol. II, A.A. Macdonell & A.B. Keith, p. 279.

general term for all string instruments. The *Veena* in later *Samhitas* and *Brahmanas* denotes a lute. According to *Satpatha Brahmna*, an instrument like *Vana* having one hundred strings (*Shatatantu*), used to be played during *Mahavrata rite*.[1] The *Vana* or *Maha* had all strings of *Munja* (grass) and was played with two bamboo pieces. There were ten holes in the *Dada* of the instrument and from each emerged ten strings. Thirty three of these were fixed by the *Advaryu*, (an officiating priest) and a equal number each by the *hota* (the sacrifical priest who chanted the *Rig-Veda*) and the *Udgata* (the priest who chanted the *Sama-Veda*). The final one was tied by the *Yajamana* (the house-holder), who was the patron of sacrifice. In later literature this instrument is generally equated with the *Shatatantri Veena*[2]. In *Rig-Veda* we find also ref. to seven notes (*Dhatus*), which are also called seven *Vanis* of the instrumental music.[3] The Vedic notes went by the names of *Krusta, Prathama, Dvitiya, Tritiya, Caturtha, Mandra and Atsvarya* and were known as *saptha dhatus* or seven notes. They were produced in 100 string *Veena*. *Rik-Samhita* has been accepted as one of the earliest books. Here we find mentioned the names of various types of *Veena* and their sizes. The *Veenas* were named variously according to shape and size viz. *Shoni, Picchola or Picchori, Aghati, Ghatalika, Nadi, Vanaspati, Oudumburi, Kandaveena, Vana or Satatantri, Veena, Karkari, Pinga, Apaghatalika, Aisiki and Kashvapi or Kacchapi* [4]. The *Veena* of the same type has been seen to have more than one name; for instance, the harp with seven strings had more than one name - the *Chitra*, the *Parivadini* and the *Saptatantri Veena*. Since detailed information about these is lacking, it is difficult to say whether they were different except in the number of strings or whether

1. Vedic Index, Vol. II, A.A. Macdonell & A.B. Keith, p. 316
2. Deva B.C., 'Musical Instruments', p. 81.
3. Macdonell's Vedic Grammar - ' Macdonell', p. 64
4. Goswami O, 'The story of Indian Music', p. 293.

they were the same instrument but known by various names in different regions. *Chitra* was the best known and is referred to in the Ramayana on many occasions.[1]

Veena has certain iconographic and occult significances. It is supposed to be the instrument of Goddess Saraswati; Goddess of *Veena Pustaka Dharini*; one who holds the divine source of sound and wisdom. In Ramayana, Valmiki has also mentioned about a very ancient *Veena* like *Vipanchi* and it seems like at that period only seven *Shuddha Jaatis* were in vogue and fretted instruments, like *Kinnari*, were not invented then. From it also we come to know that *Gandharva* and *Yuddha-Sangeet* (martial song) and also a different type of *Gandharva* music which was mainly concerned with the common people was also prevalent in those days.[2] In Naradi Shiksha we find Narada has referred both to the *Veena* and *Venu*. He has equated the *Veena* with *Vedic* music and *Venu* with *Gandharva* or popular one, thus giving the *Veena* a hallowed place in the musical hierarchy of India.[3]

Next we come to *Jatakas* or legends of the Buddha's previous birth. In them we find the frequent mention of the *Veena*, the *Venu* and the Mridanga. The birth stories of *Jatakas* of Gautam Buddha, were compiled sometime between 3rd & 2nd Century B.C. At the end of 3rd Century B.C., these stories were held to be sacred by orthodox Buddhists, and they were chosen as the subjects to be represented round the most sacred Buddhist buildings, e.g. in the relics of shrines at *Sanchi*, Amaravati, Barhut etc. and they were popularly known under the name of *Jataka*. The number of *Jatakas* are 547 or 550 or 565 and of them the *Veenasthuna* and *Guptila Jatakas* in particular contain references about the musical instruments like the *Veena*, *Venu* etc. It has been mentioned in

1. Deva B.C. 'Musical Instruments', p. 82.
2. Dr. Sharmistha Sen's Thesis.
3. Goswami O, 'The Story of Indian Music, p. 294.

the *Guptila-Jataka* that *Guptila* a and *Musila* used to play the Veena, having seven strings.[1]

In Vedic and Buddhist literature different kinds of *Veena* have been mentioned and the authors like Narada. Bharata, Matanga, Parsvadeva and Sarangdeva (early 13th Century A.D.) as well as most of the post - Sarangdeva writers of music, have described the characteristics of different kinds of *Veena* in their respective works.[2]

Narada, author of Sangit Makaranda, has referred to eighteen types of *Veena* viz Kacchapi or Kashapi, Kubjika, Chitra, Paribaaini Nakuli, Mahati, Jaya, Vaishnavi, Roudri, Barani, Saraswati, Kinnari, Kurmi, Sourandhri, Ghoshaka, Bhanati, Joshtha & Brahni. Except for Mahati,Saraswati, Rouduri, and Kacchapi all these have passed into the womb of time. Kinnari is the instrument still used by some of the trible people in India. Saraswati Veena is used in South India but Kacchapi Veena, though found in North India is becoming rare. The Mahati *Veena* otherwise known as veena in the North, is the one referred to in almost all of our Upanishads, Puranas and Sanskrit dramas. Even in the older times it had acquired such sanctity that Yagnavalkaya, one of the foremost of ancient law-givers says, "He who knows the art of *Veena* playing and *Shruti Shastra* & *Tala* can attain God easily".

Its sound is thought to be closest to the human voice, capable of producing almost all its shades and variations.[3] Another interesting example is the inscription of harps on coins, the best known example is the coin of Samudra Gupta.

All string instruments are thought to have been derived from *Veena* In any string instument still there is something of *Veena* which exists even at present. The first to come out of veena is supposed to be *Santoor*, which is characteristics of the Kashmir Valley and was neither seen nor played

1. Prajanananda Swami, 'A Historical Study of Indian Music', pp. 114-115
2. Ibid., p. 114.
3. Goswami O, "The Story of Indian Music', p. 295.

anywhere else except that lately Film Industry has adopted it on a large scale. Some scholars are of the opinion that this instrument can be traced to *Vedic Vana Veena. Satatanstri Veena* had hundred strings of spun grass which name got modified to *Santoor*, which has sixty number of strings and is struck with sticks. The other type of instrument of this family is *Swarmandal* which is similar to qanoon a west Asian instrument as mentioned in Ain-I-Akbari. It has twenty one strings. After around 10th Century A.D. the polychords almost vanished from the Indian scene except the *Santoor* and the *Svaramandal*. "The monochords or finger-board instruments like the *Kacchapi*, the *Rabab*, the *Sarode*, the *Sitar*, the *Saraswati Veena*, which are lutes and the *Kinnari* and *Rudra Veena* which are zithers take over and dominate the musical realm. A system based on harps is given up and a new one founded or fingerboard *Veenas* leading to our present practice, replacing the older music".[1]

Regarding the present day construction of *Veena*, it is mostly made in Tanjore and Mysore in South and Miraj in Western India. In Tanjore it is made of jackwood, while in Mysore blackwood is used. The instrument consists of a large pea-shaped bowl hollowed out of one piece of wood. The side string bridge is secured to the main bridge and the belly[2]. The bridge is wide and is covered at the top with a plate of metal. Over this run four strings which go on to four pegs at the farther end, which is in the shape of the mythical animal, Yali. Besides the main bridge, and attached to it is a subsidiary metallic one over which pass three thin strings, the *Sarani*. The Veena of North India has two gourds on which is fixed a bamboo or wooden tube which is the *dandi* or finger board. At one end is the wide bridge of ivory, wood or horn and frets are fixed by means of wax on to the *dandi*. *Raga's*

---

1. Deva. B.C. 'Musical Instruments', p. 86.
2. Popley A. Herbert, 'The Music of India', p. 105.

are played on four main strings of metal; besides these there are also subsidiary over for *drone* and *jhala*..[1]

Only *Alap* consisting of 18 divisions is played on the Veena which are known as :

(1) Asthai varnam (2) Antara Varnam (3) Sanchari Varnam (4) Bhog Varnam (5) Abhog Varnam (6) Barabar Ki Jod (7) Gamak Jod (8) Ladi Jod (9) Jhala (10) Thonk (11) Kattar Jhar (12) Ladi (13) Lal-Guthav (14) Lad-Lapet (15) Paran (16) Sath Sangat (17) Dhun (18) Matha.

The first five divisions of Alap follow Vilambit *Laya* (slow tempo) but without *Tala*, and the next three in *Madhya Laya* (medium tempo) and last ten in Druta or fast tempo with *Tala* or beats.[2] There are two main styles of playing the Veena. One is the common *Tar-Paran* Technique and the other is the performance of *dhrupada* compositions on the *Veena*.

CONTRIBUTION TO VEENA BY SENIA'S

The descendants of Misri Singh S/o Maharaja Samokhan Singh and his wife Saraswati Devi, the daughter of Tansen, formed the main *Gharana* of *Veena* Music. They used to sing *Dhrupadas* in both Dagar and *Khandar Bani*.

Although the *Veena* has now come to be regarded as a solo instrument, it may be interesting to note that in ancient times, *Veena* was used more as an instrument for accompanying the singers. Even during the Mughal period, *Beenkars*, as a rule, accompanied the singers. In point of fact a solo performance on the *Veena*, was then frowned upon by the musicians, so much so, that it was called *Shushka-Vadya* i.e. dry instrumental music. It is generally believed that great *Veena* player, Naubat Khan (Misri Singh) was seldom asked to

1. Deva B.C., 'Indian Music', pp. 135 & 138.
2. Goswami O, 'The Story of Indian Music', p. 297.

give solo recitals in the Court of Akbar. He usually accompanied Tansen on *Veena*. Before establishing itself as a solo instrument, it was being used as an accompanying instrument. The *Veena* adopted itself to the style of *Dhrupada Ang Alap* which preceded a *Dhrupada* recital. It was capable of producing all the intricate embellishments of the Vocal Alap.

In Tansen's life sketch as well as in *Dhrupada Vanis* have been discussed. The Classical instrumental Music of Northern India was also developed on the same lines.

Although between Misri Singh and Niyamat Khan not much is known about the *Veena* players, except that all people in the line of Misri Singh were *Veena* players and used to accompany the vocalists, but at the same time, they have all worked for progress of *Veena* Both the descendants of Bilas Khan as well as Misri Singh used to play on *Veena* They were in close contact with each other all along. It was Niyamat Khan (Sadarang), in the line, to popularise the *Veena* and make it a solo instrument. Niyamat Khan also formed the famous *Kawwal Gharana*. The descendants of Niyamat Khan, along with the descendants of Bilas Khan, who were attached to the Court of Lucknow, used to play on *Rabab* and *Veena*.

Later, during the time of Muhammad Shah Rangila, we find reference to Niyamat Khan (Sadarang) accompanying Gulab Khan on *Veena*.[1] Incidently Niyamat Khan was a direct descendant of Naubat Khan and was a great *Beenkar*. A *Khayal* composed by Manarang gives a clear indication of his mastery over the instrument.[2] It appears that Sadarang being a creative artiste, was keen on proving his mettle as a solo-player as this would give him the scope for displaying his virtuosity. He also felt that the instrumentalist did not get the

---

1. Acharaya Sudarshan, 'Sangit Sudarshan, p. 18.
2. Bhatkhande V.N. Kramik-Pustaq-Malika', p. 226

same recognition like the vocalist. Sadarang is also credited with inventing Khayal within the framework of *Dhrupada*. It is believed that after Muhammad Shaha Rangila listened to *Khayal* he was so pleased with Sadarang that he permitted him to give solo performance on the *Veena* at his court. It is said that from that time onwards the Veena became a solo instrument.

During the later part of the eighteenth Century Nirmal Shah, grand son of Bhupat Khan (Manarang), was a great Veena Player representing the line of Misri Singh Ji. He made Varanasi as his home after leaving Delhi. Jafar Khan who was descendant in the line of Bilas Khan and was closely related to Nirmal Shah, was not able to compete with Nirmal Shah in Courts of Lucknow and Kashi because of masterly display of Nirmal Shah which had no parallel in *'Vilambita Alap'* and *Jhala*. In order to equal the charms of *Veena*, Jafar Khan invented new instrument of *Sur-Sringara*, which even was highly appreciated by Nirmal Shah the *Veenkar*.

After the death of Nirmal Shah his brother's son Umrao Khan, who was son of Chote Noubat Khan and was given the title of Rasbin Khan Rangaran, took up the position of the great *Veena* player of his time. It was he who invented *'Surbahar'*. It is said that Umrao Khan on Veena could compete with Pyar Khan on *Sursringar*. They mostly used to give subsequently friendly duets. During this period Sadak Ali Khan son of Jafar Khan, although a great musicologist and excellent in Rabab, was very efficient in *Veena* also. Although authors like Sudarshan Acharya have dubbed him as a proudly person, but he taught *Veena* also to his disciples like Mahesh Chandra Sarkar and Methailallji, besides teaching *Dhrupada*, *Rabab* and *Sitar* to many persons. It is reported by Birendra Kishore Roy Chaudhuri that when Shri Ramkrishna Paramahansadev visited Varanasi on pilgrimage, and listened to the Veena of Mahesh Chandra Sarkar, he got absorbed in "Samadhi".

After the death of Sadak Ali Khan, Ali Muhammad Khan the eldest son of Sangeet Nayak Basat Khan was appointed by the Raja of Varanasi as the Chief Musician of his court. He imparted the lessons on the vocal music of *Dhrupada* and instrumental music on *Veena* and *Sur-Sringar* to the great Veena player, Wazir Khan Saheb of Rampur (1861-1926 A.D.). With the death of Ali Muhammad, *Veena* gradually disappeared from Varanasi. The last great *Veena* player at Varanasi was late Mithailallji.

After Umrao Khan, his son Amir Khan *veenkar's* concentration, although originally an instrumentalist, remained on vocal Music. In the Rampur Darbar he seldom played on *Veena* in the presence of Bahadur Hussain Khan, who was his uncle-in-law. Bahadur Hussain Khan who was a nephew of Pyar Khan Seni and Amir Khan founded the Rampur *gharana*. Amir Khan was characterised by some special charms in the use of *Alap, Dhrupad, Dhamar* in the veena which were not found anywhere in India. They both gave theoretical and practical knowledge of music to Nawab Haider Ali Khan a brother of the then ruling Nawab of Rampur. Among the disciples who got initiated in *Veena* by these musicians were Muhammad Hussain, Nabi Bakash and Ali Hussain.

After Amir Khan the great *Veenkar* was his son Wazir Khan. He learnt *Veena* from his father and Basat Khan and *Sur-Sringar* from Bahadur Hussain. Wazir Khan built up the musical career of Pramathanath Bandopadyaya (*Rudra Veena*) and Mohammad Hussain in *Veena*. Wazir Khan, a gem of Rampur Court and a celebrated maestro of *Been* produced innumerable noted artists, including Ustad Allauddin Khan and Ustad Hafiz Ali Khan.[1] Wazir Khan gave lessons to the Nawab of Rampur who was himself a great exponent of classical music. The Nawab held Wazir Khan in very high esteem and adorned him with many decorations.

1. Aggarwal Vinay Kumar, "Trends & Traditions", p. 36.

After Wazir Khan his son Sagir Khan adopted *Veena* and imparted training to Mukhopadyaya and to Shri Birendra Kishore Roy Chaudhuri although Birendra Kishore Roy Chaudhuri had also training under Dabir Khan who was son of Nazir Khan and grandson of Wazir Khan. Sagir Khan did not take music seriously and went to Pakistan.[1] Dabir Khan was one of the great *Veena* Players and Guru of Shri Birendra Kishore Roy Chaudhuri, both of whom have passed away now. With their passing away there are not any renowned Veena players left out of Senia *Gharana*.

According to Ustad Rahimuddin Khan Dagur, Dabir Khan and Shri Birendra Kishore Roy Chaudhuri's *Alap* has twelve or thirteen main divisions depending on the *Laya* or rhythm in which they are rendered. According to Sh. Birendra Kishore Roy Chaudhuri there are 364 *bols* of *Veena*. *Thok Jhala* of *Veena* is derived from the Tantric Mantra Chant etc. In *Veena* there are 360 *bols* according to Acharya Brahaspati.[2] Nawab Haider Ali Khan got these *bols* from Bahadur Hussain Khan after paying him one Lakh rupees. Another *Beenkar* was Ustad Sadiq Ali Khan, who was the son of the illustrious *Beenkar* Musharaff Khan of Alwar, who was unrivalled in his times. Sadiq Ali Khan was attached to Rampur Darbar.

Presently among the great *Veenkars* is Ustad Asad Ali Khan. Asad Ali Khan is the son of Late Ustad Sadiq Ali Khan of Rampur but as per Asad Ali Khan, his ancestors follow the *Khandari Vani* which was perfected to suitably applied to *Veena* by Rajab Ali Khan and Musharaff Khan and claim their descendance from Nayak Bakshu of the time of Raja Maan Singh Tomar of Gwalior, Asad Ali Khan excells in different techniques on the *Veena* and plays a variety of *gamakas* and *Chhut Tanas* with masterly perfection.

Abdul Aziz Khan of Patiala, his younger brothers

1. Personal interview with Shri Birendra Kishore Roy Chaudhuri.
2. Acharaya Brahaspati, p. 541.

Habib Khan and Alla Diya Khan were the great exponents of the instrument.[1] Other noteworthy and living artists are Gopal Krishan (who took lessons from Pandit Ravi Shankar also), Lal Mani Mishra (Reader in Instrumental Music, Banaras University) and Ahmad Raza (disciple of abdul Aziz Khan). Both Gopal Krishna and Ahmad Raza are on the staff of A.I.R. New Delhi.[2]

But the fact remains that *Veena* has gradually disappeared along with *Dhrupad*. In Northern India, we hardly hear *Been* from the Artists excepting a few whose names have been given above.

1. Aggarwal Vinay Kumar, 'Trends & Traditions', p. 36
2. Ibid..

CHAPTER VI

RABAB : ITS EVOLUTION AND THE CONTRIBUTION OF SENIA'S IN IT

Rabab was introduced to Hindustani Music around the 14th Century and continued to be a popular stringed instrument during the early Mughal period. Its contribution and shape, however, went under some changes in keeping with the requirements of stylized classical music.

It is difficult to ascertain whether Rabab is an indigenous or a foreign instrument. According to some musicologists, it is a modified form of *Rudra Veena*, which, when travelled Westward came to be known as *Rabab* in the Arabian Countries and *Rebec* in Europe.[1]

The author of "Kamus" writes about the origin of Rabab that 1,000 years ago a person named Abdullah of village, Basud, invented this instrument and gave it the name of Rabab.[2]

The Sikh Historians in general, are of the opinion that the Rabab was invented by Guru Nanak, which his chief attendant and disciple Bhai Mardana used to play with the *Vanis* and *Shabadas* of Guru.[3] In another book Quanoon-I-Mausiqui, Sadiq Ali Khan refers to the Rabab as an instrument which was played during the time of Guru Nanak. According to him the instrument was invented and developed by Guru Nanak Shah. This Rabab contained six strings only.[4] But according to "Khalsa Twarikh Puratan

---

1. Tagore Surinder Mohan, 'Yantra Kosh', p. 27.
2. Bekta Firozabadi Majad Aldin - 'Kamus'.
3. Surinder Mohan, "Yantra Kosh", p. 27.
4. Khan Sadiq Ali, 'Quanoon-I-Mausiqui', p. 309.

Janam", the Rabab is an Arab instrument which Guru Nanak remodelled into a new form. It also says that it was made under the Guru's instructions by a designer named Firande and was presented to Bhai Mardana by the Guru.[1]

From the historical point of view, it would be wrong to maintain that the Rabab was invented by Guru Nanak. This is an Arab musical instrument which came into popular vogue with the advent of the Turks in India. In India the instrument like Rabab was previously played with a bow, but the shape of that Rabab was very much different from the classical Rabab. It resembled small sized wooden Sarode. Such type of Rabab is still popular as a folk instrument of Kashmir. In Kashmir, Rabab is particularly used with the*Soofiana and Chhakri*. Rabab is popular in Punjab region also, but it is now played with a plectrum, unlike all other Rababs of the world which are played with a bow.

A great scholar, Captain C.R. Day, writes that the Rebec, once popular in Europe, was a form of the Rabab, brought to spain by the Moors, who in turn had derived it from Persia and Arabia. Here again, the Aryan origin of Rabab is evident.[2]

He has stated that this Rabab resembles the *Tanbur* of Khurasan, a long necked lute having a small buldging body, several frets on the finger board and two strings of the same thickness which were plucked with a plectrum.

In his description, Al-Farabi does not give a difinite information as to whether this Rabab was plucked with a plectrum or played with a bow, although he mentions the resembling instrument *Tanbur* having been plucked.

It would thus appear that the term Rabab denotes bowed instruments in general and more so, because it signifies a stringed instrument played with a bow. It also corresponds to the Persian word (Kamanca, probably derived from Kaman (bow), which in Persia denotes especially the spike fiddle, and which too can be used as

---

1. Paintal Dr. A.S. Doctoral Thesis on the topic of the Nature and Place of music in Sikh Religion and its affinity with Hindustani Classical Music, Delhi University 1971,.p. 312.
2. Captain C.R. Day - The Musical instruments of Southern India and Deccean, p. 103.

a general term for bowed instruments as well. (It will be of interest to note that even now there exists a folk instrument called (Kamaicha in Rajasthan). This is a bowed instrument played like Sarangi by a class of professional singers called Manghniars for Vocal accompaniment.

It may not be wrong to assume, therefore, that the Rabab originally was a bowed instrument. There appears to be little or no progressive development made on this instrument since its origin. No illustration of the long necked and bowed lute as described by Al-Farabi has so far been found, and as such, it may be assumed that this type of Rabab, if it at all existed, had very short span of life. But those forms of Rabab and Kamanca which were already known in the 10th and 11th Century, are still in use and from these other bowed instruments have evolved.

H.A. Popley describes, "It is a handsome instrument and has a very pleasing tone, fuller than that of Sarangi. It lends itself to the graces better than the Sitar as it has no frets".[1] According to Surinder Mohan Tagore, vide his famous book "Yantra Kosh", it consists of a large piece of hollowed wood or stern, supported at the bottom by a circular wooden belly which is also hollowed out and covered with sheep skin (*khal*). A wooden bridge placed on the middle of the belly, called *Ghuruk* and another placed on top, called *Tar-Gahar*, are used for the support of the six strings used in Rabab. These six strings are known as *Rodas*. These are attached to the extreme lower portion. The sheep skin (*khal*) covering the belly is also called *Mand*. The flat wooden finger board is called *Asthana* the Rabab has no side strings or *Chikaris*. As the finger board is of wood, metal strings are not used, only catgut is used in Rabab.

The Rabab is a fretless instrument. It suffers from certain limitations and does not lend itself to *Vilambit-Alap* as no steel strings are used on its finger board. The instrument is, therefore, more suitable to rhythmic elaboration than for melodic improvisation. It would thus appear that *Madhya-Jod* portion in enhanced speed, can be rendered on this instrument well, which in other words

1. Popley H.A., Music of India, p. 14.

means that it is more suitable for *Nauharvani.*

Rabab used by Senia's as a Classical Musical Instrument

Rabab formerly was a very popular folk instrument of North India. The instrument gained popularity in Bengal as well as in the temples of Bankura, Bishnupur and Surat.

Probably from the time of Tansen it became a stylised classical instrument. According to some Musicologists Tansen is credited with the invention of Rabab.[1] There is, however, historical evidence to show that an instrument very much like Rabab existed even during Babar's time. Tansen was, however, responsible for raising it to the status of a classical instrument. Tansen was known as the best Rabab player also.

Tansen's descendants called themselves *Rababiyas* in order to distinguish themselves from the descendants of Tansen's daughter's line who were known as *Beenkaras*, till lately. Tansen's descendants kept up the tradition by playing Rabab only for its sanctified or distinguished associations with Tansen.

With the decline of Mughal Empire, the Senia's or the descendants of Tansen left Delhi and one section migrated to the East while the other, to the West. The Eastern migrators were called *Poorabiyas*, while those settled in the West under the patronage of Rajput princess were called *Pachaos* or *Westerners*.[2] Most of the *Rababiyas* and *Beenkaras* Senia *Gharana* who migrated to the East settled at Banaras and nearby places, under the patronage of Hindu and Muslim rulers like the Naresh of Banaras, Nawab of Oudh, Rajas of Betia and Rewa, Nawab of Rampur state, all of whom were not only great patrons of music but also musicians themselves.

After Tansen there were many famous exponents of Rabab in Tansen's line. Among them Chharju Khan's sons, Jafar Khan, Pyar Khan and Basat Khan, were famous Rabab players. It is said by Shri Birendra Kishore Roy Chaudhuri that Jafar Khan used to play duet with Nirmal Shah, brother of Chharju Khan. Basat Khan was a

1. Popley H.A., Music of India, p. 18
2. Roy Chaudhuri Birendra Kishore, Indian Music & Mian Tansen, p. 18.

contemporary and the Court Musician of Nawab Wazid Ali Shah of Lucknow and accompanied the Nawab to Matiaburj, Calcutta, where he became very famous. Jafar Khan's grandson Kasim Ali (son of Kazim Ali), was one of the greatest *Rababiyas* of his family. Kasim Ali had his training in Rabab, Sur-Sringar and Dhrupad from Basat Khan of Senia *Gharana*.

Kasim Ali was a great favourite of Raja Surinder Mohan Tagore.[1] Jafar Khan's Son, Sadiq Ali Khan, was a leading Rabab player. He became attached to the Court of the Raja of Varanasi. Shri Birendra Kishore Roy Chaudhuri states that Sadiq Ali Khan was a great Musicologist and excelled in Rabab. Bahadur Sen or Khan, Pyar Khan's sister's son, was the celebrated Rabab player as well as Sur-Sringar player. Although he was a Dhrupad singer also, but he concentrated more on the Instrumental Music and had such a charming style of play that people used to say that his fingers were made of diamonds. Not only the lovers of classical music, but even uninitiated laymen were overwhelmed with rapturous joy by the sound of his instrumental displays. He introduced many new *Alankars* in the instrumental music.[2]

Pyar Khan remained bachelor and taught Rabab and Sur-Sringar to Bahadur Sen.[3]

Basat Khan had two sons, Ali Muhammad Khan and Muhammad Ali Khan, they both were leading Rabab players.

Ali Muhammad Khan, the eldest son of Basat Khan, was appointed by the Raja of Varanasi as the chief musician of his Court.[4]

According to Birendra Kishore Roy Chaudhuri, Ali Muhammad Khan was a very liberal minded musician and used to play on his instrument before his disciples without any reservation. He had profound knowledge of Ragas and could develop any Raga, for hours without any repetitions of *Tanas*. He trained many students. He also imparted lessons in the Vocal Music of Dhrupada and Instrumental

1. Roy Chaudhuri Birendra Kishore, 'Indian Music & Mian Tansen', p. 19.
2. Ibid., p. 23.
3. Ibid. p. 24
4. Ibid. , p. 23

Music to Wazir Khan Saheb of Rampur, who during his early youth visited Varanasi frequently to meet Ali Muhammad Khan, who was related to him closely.[1]

Basat Khan's second son Muhammad Ali Khan, was the last descendant of Tansen to have played Rabab. He belonged to the family of Tansen's youngest son Bilas Khan, and in his old agesettled down in Rampur state. He was well versed in Dhrupad, he specialised in playing *Alap* in Dhrupad style on the Rabab.

Muhammad Ali Khan, the younger brother of Ali Muhammad Khan, who used to stay at Gaya, frequently visited his elder brother for lessons on Rabab. Sh.Birendra Kishore Roy Chaudhuri writes that both these brothers outshone all other famous musicians of that period who used to visit Varanasi.

Among his famous pupils were Nawab Sadat Ali Khan of Rampur (popularly known as Chhaman Sahab), Hihari lal of Gaya, Kanhaiya Lal, Shri Briendra Kishore Roy Chaudhuri and Muhammad Ali Khan's adopted son Saukat Ali Khan who died in March, 1972.

After the death of Ali Muhammad Khan and Muhammad Ali Khan, the greatest vacuum in the sphere of classical music of Varanasi could not be filled up. The remaining few musicians of Tansen's tradition were settled in the states of Rampur and Jaipur.

It is a great pity that with the disappearance of the descendants of Tansen the culture of Dhrupada, Been and Rabab gradually disappeared and the musicians of *Senia Gharana* who settled in Jaipur got interested in playing sitar.

The tunning system as followed by the established *Rababiyas* of *Senia gharana* is given below :

The first string from the left is tuned to *Pa* of *Madhya Saptak*, the second is tuned to *Re* of *Mandra Saptak*, the third to *Sa* of *Mandra Saptak* the fourth to *Pa* of *Mandra Saptak* and last the 6th string to *Sa of Madhya Saptak*.[2]

The Rabab players call these strings *Neer, Mian, Surr,*

1. Roy Chaudhuri Birendra Kishore, 'Indian Music & Mian Tansen', p. 24.
2. Tagore Surindra Mohan, 'Yantra Kosh', p. 27

Mandra, Ghor and *Kharaj.*[1]

Rabab, in view of its limitations, is more suited to *Madhya Jod Alap* rather than *Vilambit Alap* in which various nuances are employed with *Gamaka, Chhut*,., *Chapak, Tar-Paran* and *Ladi* etc. Shri Birendra Kishore Roy Chaudhuri stated that it is right hand which plays the more important role in Rabab playing. The Chhapak technique is produced by means of left hand finger nails which strike blow on the strings, thus producing sound less metallic than that of other stringed instruments played with plectrum giving almost a resemblance of the human voice.[2]

The right hand technique excels in *Madhya-Alap, Ladi, Jod* and *Paran*.. Due to its structural advantages, the *Sut* technique can easily be applied to the Rabab.

Raja Surinder Mohan Tagore mentions that Rabab players used to tie a strong scale of fish to the left index finger which would glide over the string. Even now, some Sarode players either grow long nails on their index fingers or fix strong fish scales with some sort of addesive to their fingers.

The strings are plucked with the help of a triangular shaped plectrum called *Java* made of Sandal wood or Bamboo Coconut shell, held between the index finger and the thumb of the right hand.

According to Shri Birendra Kishore Roy Chaudhuri the main *bol* of the Rabab is *Da* produced by plucking the strings in other directions. The same technique is being followed in Sur-Sringar and Sarode.

Most of the modern musicians are hardly acquainted with Rabab which has become almost extinct today. The instrument was confined only to the descendants of Tansen and to those only who came into close contact with them and also learnt from them.

---

1. Personal Communications with Shri Birendra Kishore Roy Chaudhuri.
2. Ibid.

CHAPTER VII

KHAYAL : ITS EVOLUTION AND CONTRIBUTION TO IT BY SENIA'S

The Khayal today is the most popular classical form of Vocal Music in North India. The world *Khayal* or *Khyal* (Khayal in Bengali and Khyal in Hindi and Urdu) seems to be an Arabic term, meaning thought imagination fancy, idealion, imaginative conception, respect, understanding etc., and it also connotes the idea of some sort of song in imaginative and thoughtful verse. The term Khayal is often used to convey the same meaning as the word *Dhyan* (meditation in Hindi). But in the field of music, this word refers to a specific form of music. In comparison with the Dhrupada Prabandha type of songs, the Khayal Prabandha is imaginative and creative, whereas Dhrupada is concentrative, contemplative and majestic.[1]

According to some scholars the word *Khayal* has been derived from the Hindi word *Khel*. In due course, this word was changed and used as Khayal in local languages.[2]

Following are few examples :

कंत बीस लोचन बिलोकिये कुमंत फल

ख्याल लाई लंका कवि रांड़ की सी झौंपरी (तुलसी - कवितावली)

कूदि पड़े चढ़ि कदम तै तुम खेलत यह ख्याल (सूरदास - सूरसागर)

सुनहु सूर वह करनि कहनि यह ऐसे प्रभु के ख्याल (सूरदास-सूरसागर)

चकृत नर नारी करत खयाला (सूरदास - सूरसागर)

Here is another example of song in which the word khel has been used as Khayal :

---

1. Swami Prajanananda, "The Historical Study of Indian Music", p. 202.
2. Shukla Dr. S., "Khayal Ek Punaravalokan Sangeet", January - February, 1976.

घमार राग सिन्दूरा (आगरा घराना)
लाल तुम नए नए खयाल खेलन लागे
कैसे बचेंगे बृज बाल[1]

In Rajashthan some particular paintings depicting the incidents of historical events are also called Khayal. Some *Lavni* (Folk music) singers describe in their songs some historical stories and play *Chhang* (an instrument) in their accompaniment, and they call these songs Khayal[2]. Sufis, like Shah Burhanuddin, composed songs describing the anguish or pain of love and called them Khayal[3]. In Sufism the mystic songs, which were composed as Ghazals praising *Peers* (Saints) and prophets, were also described as Khayal. In this way Ghazal and Khayal and also Qawwali belong to the same category of music. These Khayal singers called it *Banda* or *Langra Dhrupad*. In other words, we can say that Khayal singers gave an answer to the Dhrupad.[4]

A special variety of musical poems which are recited by the Sufi saints in Southern India is also known as Khayal. The nature of these songs is music.[5]

In Raag Darpana, Faqirullah has mentioned about a special type of musical instrument named Khayal during the time of Shah Jehan. This Instrument was invented by Sheikh Bahauddin.[6]

Regarding the Origin of Khayal there are many controversies among the scholars of Indian Music. Since the authors do not give any authentic historical evidence in support of their opinion, it is very difficult to come to a definite conclusion. Still there are various theories which have been advanced in this regard.

Some are of the opinion that some wandering Qawwal singers were already in existence in different parts of Northern India, even before the time of Sultan Alauddin Khilji and Amir Khusro, who lived in the 13th & 14th

---

1. Collection of Dr. (Mrs.) Sumati Mutatkar.
2. Acharya Brahaspati, "Musalman", Ghazal, Qawwali Aur Khayal", p. 61.
3. Acharya Brahaspati, "Musalman Aur Bhartiya Sangeet", p. 112.
4. Ibid.
5. Ibid., p. 113.
6. Faqirullah,"Raag Darpan", p. 19.

Century A.D. during Sultan Alauddin's reign. Some musicologists are of opinion that the result of admixture of decorative principle and word structure of melody gave rise to the new and novel form of Khayal. Some hold that from the musical composition (*Prabandha*) *Kaivada*, possessed of three musical parts (*Dhatus*) and (*Bhavani Jati*) with three limbs (*Angas*) of the 12th & 13th Century A.D. evolved the new form of *Khayal*.[1] Some scholars are again of the opinion that not only *Kaivada* but other *Prabandha's* like *Ekatali* and *Rasaka* are also the fountain head of *Khayal*. Some others again argue that Khayal was designed after the *Sastric Aksiptika*, which has been described by Sharangdeva in the *Sangit Ratnakara*.[2] He connected it with the kind of Nibandha Gaan pertaining to *Margi Sangeet*. It was a composition which was sung with the help of *Tala*, *Swara* and *Pada* such as *Chanchat-Putta Tal* which seems to be a variety of *Marga Talas*. Some musicologists are of the opinion that the musical composition is set in a particular *Raag-Tal*, and also contains *Pada*, the literary content. In this manner it embodies all the elements of Khayal style.

Apart from the above opinions, the most notworthy thought is that the origin of Khayal style may be related to our ancient *Geetis*, particularly to *Sadharni Geeti*. *Geeti* was considered in the system or manner involved in the style of musical composition and rendering.

The authors of *Madunul Mausiqui Sarmaya-E-Isharat, Marrifun-Nagmat* and many more writers are of the opinion that sultan Hussain Sharqui year 1485 A.D. of Jounpur was a founder of the Khayal style.[3]

Fox Strangways and Captain Willard are also of the opinion that Sultan Hussain Sharqui was the great master of the art of music and he was the founder of Khayal style.

Inayat Khan Rasik has mentioned that Sultan Hussain was an expert singer of Qawwali and some of his compositions are available in *Khairabadi* language.[4] According to Pandit V.N. Bathkhandey it is not correct to

---

1. Swami Prajanananda, "A Historical Study of Indian Music", p. 203.
2. Sarangdeva, "Sangeet Ratnakara".
3. Hakim Karam Imam,"Madunul Mausiqui", Sarmaya-E-Ishrat Marrifun-Naghmat".
4. Khan Inayat Rasikh, "Risala-E-Zikre - Mughannian-E-Hindustan", p. 24.

believe that any single person could have originated and developed the Khayal style. He says that musical compositions similar to Khayal already existed in the society, but they did not have due recognition and appreciation by the people at that time. Later, in the fifteenth Century, Sultan Hussain Sharqui took a fancy for it and encouraged the musicians to sing in this style, which might have given impetus to its development and popularity.[1]

Another modern musicologist, Swami Prajanananda, is of the opinion that Sharqui rulers were great lovers, as well as patrons of fine Arts like Architecture, Painting and Music, and so it can be assumed that Khayal got their support and was understood and much improved during the time of Sultan Hussain Sharqui.[2]

Acharya Brahaspati states that the independent ruler, Ibrahim Sharqui (1404-1440 A.D.), was a very knowledgeable person. Sultan Hussain who also belonged to Sharqui dynasty, was a great connoisseur of music and also a contemporary of Man Singh Tomar of Gwalior. Famous singers like Sheikh Adhan (Sufi Musician) Sheikh Bhanju (who once challanged Tansen in Akbar's court) and Ghooran were all from Jaunpur. Thus all these muscicians from Jaunpur were called *Qawwal Bachchay*, and they were always in conflict with the Kalawants, who believed in the purity of Ragas.[3]

Thakur Jaidev Singh is of the opnion that Sultan Hussain Sharqui cannot be said to be the originator of this style. He states that the style of Khayal was ornate and romantic and it did not find favour in the temples. It was mostly patronised by the Kathakis, the dancing girls and kings. The Sharqui kings of Jaunpur patronised this style to a great extent. He further states that there was a certain style of musical composition, and certain style of rendering already prevalent in music and Khayal was only a natural development of that style[4]. Dr. V.K. Aggarwal writes that in 17th Century Shah Jehan's time Sheikh Bahauddin

---

1. Bhatkhande Pandit V.N. "Sangeet Shastra" , vol. I, p. 58.
2. Prajanananda Swami, "A Historical Study of Indian Music.
3. Sulochana and Brahaspati Acharya, "Khayal Sangeet", July 1979, p. 28.
4. Thakur Jaidev Singh "The Evolution of Khayal, Commemoration Volume in Honour of Dr. S.N. Ratanjankar, 1961, pp. 127-132.

Zakeria, a big *Pir* and spiritual leader of Multan (Originator of Rag Multani) invented a new stringed instrument and named it Khayal[1].

There are again differences of opinion regarding the innovator or originator of Khayal. Some say that the Indo-Persian scholar, Amir Khusro, was an accomplished musician as well as a musicologist and that he himself was conversant with the popular type of song, the Qawwali of the *Qawwal*. It is said that he introduced Khayal with a particular style of execution among the music loving people of them society. But most of the scholars have refused this view[2]. Amir Khusro being the man of extraordinary merit and intelligence, well versed in the Indian languages, must have been aware of the compositions described in our ancient Shastrik texts. It is also noteworthy that various ancient compositions were described in Sangeet Ratnakar which was written around the same period, it further evidences of the continuity of ancient traditions during the time of Amir Khusro[3].

In this process, the ancient Shastrik *Prabandhas*, *Rupakalapti*, *Raag Giti* were influenced by the styles like *Qawwali*, etc., and it culminated in the emergence of a new style of music which came to be known as Khayal. But it could not attain much popularity. But Sharqui kings of Jaunpur took interest in the development and popularisation of this style. However, during the fifteenth and sixteenth Century, this style did not get much encouragement. Its oblivion was due to the dominance of Dhrupada during that period[4]. Abul Fazal in his book Ain-I-Akbari has described the names of *Kalawants* (Dhrupad Singers) but he has not mentioned the names of *Qawwal* (khayal Singer). Although Khayal was not popular at the time of Emperor's reign, still we get some important works of Khayal in Brajabhasa called "*Chaurasi Vaishnao Ki Varta*". This was completed by *Shri Gokulnatha*, the grandson of Shri Vallabacharya. He mentions an interesting incident in the life of *Krishandasa Adhikari*, who was the accountant

---

1. Aggarwal Dr. V.K. , "Trends & Traditions", p. 24.
2. Swami Prajanananda,"Historical Study of Indian Music",p. 203.
3. Ahmad Najma Parveen, "Hindustani Music' , p. 120.
4. Ibid.

of Shri *Natha* temple.

'"Jaura eka Samaya Srinath Ji Ki Bhandrame-Khayal. Tappa Gayata Buti Jaura San Krisndas Bazaar Mein Tamashaya Mein Jaya Thadey Bhaya". [1] Swami Prjananananda Ji says that the passage is a long one, but he had quoted only the relevant portion which shows that Khayal was sung at that time (16th Century). Thus, it is evident that Khayal singing was much appreciated in the society during the Muhammadan period and subsequently it was warmly appreciated by the musicians as well as music lovers even during the time of Emperor Akbar, who was also an appreciater of the ornate and romantic style of Khayal, though some are of opnion that Khayal singing was not patronised by the Emperor.[2]

After that Khayal gradually attracted the minds of the beauty loving artists the later Sultans and Royal families.[3] A detailed analysis of the works of the period under study indicated that Khayal was much more popular during the seventeenth and eighteenth centuries. In Raag Darpan also we find the description of Khayal immediately after Dhrupad. The author says that it consists of two verses, but some of its composition contain four verses also.[4]

In Tohfat-ul-Hind, the topic of Khayal has been discussed soon after the Dhrupad. According to the author of Tohfat-ul-Hind, Khayal contains two verses,[5] and most of the compositions of this period are in *Khairabadi* languages.

In the book 'Madunul Mausiqui' by Karam Imam, he has mentioned the popularity of Khayal style during his period. He has also written in his book that Sultan Hussain Sharqui of Jaunpur had composed a style of singing in *Khairabadi* language with aesthetic excellence, which came to be known as Khayal and this style was very popular among the then musicians.[6]

Khayal form of music was the product of popular demand of the common sentiments. As against Dhrupad

---

1. Swami Prajanananda, 'A Historical Study of Indian Music', p. 214.
2. Ibid, p. 214.
3. Ibid. p. 214.
4. Faqirullah, 'Raag Darpan'.
5. Ansari N.H.' Tohfat-ul-Hind', Edited by N.H. Ansari.
6. Hakim Mohammad Karam Imam, 'Madunul Mausiqui'. p. 162.

it is more imaginative than technical. In this type of singing the rules are relaxed; and due to the introduction of fast *tanas*, it turns to be more imaginative. The compositions are also more romantic. The main difference between *Dhrupad* and *Khayal Gayaki* lies in the treatment of notes i.e., production of *Gamakas*, the four types of *Gamakas*, – *Zamzama*, *Gitkari*, *Khatka* and *Murki*- treating a *Raga* on the Khayal pattern, these embellishments add to the beauty of it; while the embellishments are prohibited in Dhrupad.

The form Khayal being imaginative, one can weave patterns of notes in any way in Khayal singing.

CONTRIBUTION OF SENIA'S IN KHAYAL

The political instability during the 18th Century drove many musicians from the Capital to the smaller States. In this process Khayal style took a new turn and the mystic elements in it began to be substituted by aesthetic forms in musical compositions. This new development was considerably instrumental in the popularity of Khayal during the eighteenth Century. During the same period a musician known as Niyamat Khan in the court of Mohammad Shah Rangeelay (1719-1745) was responsible in playing an important role in promoting the Khayal style.

Swami Prajanananda writes that Niyamat Khan won the title of Sadarang from Sultan Muhammad Shah for his great talents and theoretical and practical knowledge in classical music.[1] Brahaspati Ji says that Niyamat Khan got the title of Sadarang by Muhammad Shah Rangeelay in 18th Century for his great talents and theoretical and practical knowledge in Classical Music. Niyamat Khan was from the Tansen's daughters line. Shri Birendra Kishore Roy Chaudhuri states that Niyamat Khan descendant of Misri Singh husband of Saraswati Devi, Tansen's daughter is ranked as the second great musician of Indian after Tansen. He was the high priest of Muhammad Shah's Darbar and also invented new techniques of the *Veena* music and *Dharmar*.

1. Swami Prajanananda, 'A Historical Study of Indian Music', p. 214.

It is a fact that Niyamat Khan Sadarang of Tansen's line, designed the elegant classical form of Khayal in a majestic and colourful slow tempo *(Vilambit Laya)*। like Dhrupada. Swami Prajanananda further writes that he designed the Khayal either on the basis of some *SAstric Prabandha-Gitis*,, as delineated in the ancient *Sangit Sastras*, or innovated it absolutely in a new and novel form based on the somewhat reformed type of Khayal that already existed in the society. Niyamat Khan heightened the classical form of Khayal, and made it to be appreciated by the top ranking musicians and royal sovereigns of that time. Thence form, it attained the similar high position as enjoyed by *Dhrupada* and gradually came to be developed with many modifications and changes, in forms and styles, even upto the present time.

According to Inayat Khan Rasikh, Niyamat Khan was one of the greatest singers of the Dhrupada, Khayal and Tarana styles and he composed several Khayals with a high degree of perfection.[1] In his compositions his name has been given as Sadarang.[2]

Niyamat Khan Sadarang and other musicians of that time analysed the reasons for the ascendance of Dhrupad and unpopularity of Khayal. They endeavoured to incorporate the characteristics of Dhrupad into Khayal in which they were successful. Gradually this style acquired a place of great eminence in the Court, as well as a wide popularity among all classes of society due to its unique and artistic appeal.

The musicians of that time started acquiring perfection in it and introduced many innovations and experiments to please the kings and rulers.

Niyamat Khan's Khayals acquired such popularity that even today the musicians recite them, and use them as a model for new compositions.

According to Dargah Quli Khan, his (Niyamat Khan's) presence in North India is God's great gift. He was matchless in the art of music. The other speciality in him was that he did not concede to anybody's request for singing

1. Khan Inayat Rasikh, 'Risala Zikr-e-Mughannian-e-Hindustan' p. 30.
2. At the end of this Chapter his compositions have been written.

except the King's. His supreme proficiency in playing *Been* in Tansen's gharana shows that no such *Beenkar* was even born before him.

According to Mirati-e-Aftab-numa, Niyamat Khan used to compose Dhrupad, Khayal, Tarana and other styles with great maturity, freshness and colourfulness. Below are given two examples of his compositions, one of these is based on devotional and mystic sentiments, while the other is based on aesthetic and romantic sentiments[1] :

राग दरबारी

तुम साई करीम, रहीम, हकीम पाक परवरदिगार
गरबी को गरब दूर कर डारत एक छिन में
दुखियन को मोरे दाता
जो मो मन की इच्छा हो सो पूजिवो साहेब
सदारंग को दीजे दीन दुखी के दाता,

राग सूरमल्हार

आये गरजत बदरवा अति ही सुहाये
राम झून चहुं ओर तै बरसे
सदारंग अति ही सुख पाये ।

Another Khayal composer of Senia *gharana* was Feroz Khan, who has been described as the son-in-low, disciple and nephew of Niyamat Khan. Feroz Khan, known by the title of Adarang, was also an accomplished composer of Khayals of the Style of Sadarang.[2] Following one example of his compositions :

1. Collection of Dr. (Mrs.) Sumati Mutatkar.
2. See Dargah Quli Khan, Muraqqa-e-Delhi.

राग नट मल्हार

ऐ सुहागपरी कारी बदरिया
बरसन लागी अति जोर
अदारंग बूंद फुहार परन लागी
कैसे मिलूं चितचौर

Niyamat Khan Sadarang founded the famous *Kawwal Gharana* through his disciples, whom he taught classical Khayal. The *Kawwal Gharana* thus formed, was regarded as the authoritative line of *Kawwal.*[1] Shri Birendra Kishore Roy Chaudhuri states that other Gharanas like *Agra Gharana*, Gwalior Gharana of Khayal *Kirana Gharana* etc. grew up from the main *Kawwal Gharana.*[2]

In Senia Gharana after Niyamat Khan Sadarang, Adarang and Manrang there is no reference to anybody in the line of Senia's having adopted Khayal.[3] Shri Birendra Kishore Roy Chaudhuri states that during the later part of the eighteenth Century, as the financial position of the Delhi Darbar became precarious, the Seni musicians of Delhi took shelter in other Courts of India and devoted themselves more and more to the culture of Instrumental Music Sitar although they were authorities on the dhrupada songs.[4]

1. Roy Chaudhuri Birendra Kishore, 'Indian Music & Mian Tansen', p. 28.
2. Ibid.
3. Ibid.
4. Ibid., p. 29.

सदारंग कृत ख्याल, राग रामकली
झूमरा (विलम्बित)

स्थायी

ग				नि								नि	
म	गम	प	प	ध	–	प	म	प	पध	पधनि	ध	ध	प
मा	SS	छ	रि	यां	S	S	S	S	मैंS	SSS	दी	ला	गी
3							2				0		
मे				म			सा		ग		ग		
प	ग	म	(म)	रे	–	सा	ऩि	सा	रे	सा	म	–	गम
में	S	S	रे	ला	S	ल	हा	S	ध	न	की	S	SS
3							2				0		
ग				नि			प			प	म		
म	-	गमप	प	ध	–	प	नि	ध	प	गम	रे	रे	सा
हां	S	SSS	रे	कै	S	सि	ब	नी	रे	SS	लो	ग	वा
3							2				0		

अन्तरा

		नि		ध़			नि						
प	प	ध	ध	सा	सा	सा	ध	ध	सा	सा	रें	-	सां
स	दा	रं	ग	मि	लि	या	रं	ग	घु	लि	या	S	S
3				X			2				0		
सां					नि		प				ध		
नि	–	सां	-	ध	ध	प	मं	प	प	प	पध	पधनि	ध
S	S	S	S	S	मा	ई	ई	छ	S	रि	याS	SSS	S
3				X				2			0		
नि				प				नि		प	म	ग	
ध	-	प	मप	ग	-	म	ध	-	प	गम	रे	रे	सा
पू	S	जी	SS	मौ	S	S	रें	S	S	SS	म	न	की
3							2				0		

क्रमिक पुस्तक मालिका, भाग 4, पृष्ठ 330 - 331 ।

सदारंग कृत ख्याल, राग पूरियाघनाश्री - एकताल (विलबित)

स्थायी

											(प)मंप
											मेह
घ	—	प	(घ)नि	घ	—	प	(मं)प	(मं)प	(घ)मं	—	ग
बू	S	ब	नि	जां	S	मु	ह्री	न	आ	S	यां
		0		2		0		3		4	
(ग)मंरे	(ग)रेग	—	(घ)मं	—	घ	मं	ग	मं	(रे)ग	रे	सां
आ	या	S	रे	S	S	घ	र	S	में	S	रे
		0		2		0		3		4	
(घ)नि़सा	(रे)नि़	रे	ग	—	ग	(घ)मं	—	ग	मंरे	ग	(प)मप
घ	रें	S	घ	S	र	मे	S	S	रे	S	मेह
		0		2		0		3		4	

अन्तरा

(घ)मं	घ	सां	सां	सां	-	सां	सां	-	सांनि	रें	सां
आ	S	ज	सु	हा	S	ग	की	S	रा	S	त
3		4		x		0		2		0	
सां	सां	सांनि	रें	—	सां	(नि)सां	निध	रें	नि	घ	प
स	दा	S	रं	S	ग	न्या	SS	S	म	त	S
3		4				0		2		0	
(घ)मं	—घ	(ध)म	ग	(ग)मंरे	(ग)रेंग	—	(घ)मं	—	घ	(घ)मं	ग
ला	S	या	S	ला	या	S	रे	S	S	प	र
3		4				0		2		0	
मं	(रे)ग	रे	सा	(नि)सा	(रे)नि	रे	ग	—	ग	(घ)मं	—
S	मे	S	रे	अ	रे	S	घ	S	र	में	S
3		4		S		0		2		0	
ग	(मं)रे	ग	मंप								
S	रे	,	मेह								
3		4									

क्रमिक पुस्तक मालिका, भाग 4, पृष्ठ 358 - 591 ।

सदारंग कृत ख्याल, राग कामौद, त्रिताल

स्थायी

म															सा
⌐¬											प				Sका
रें	प	–	प	प	प	ध	–	प	–	–	ध	ध	प	–	प
रे	S	S	बा	ने	न	दूं	S	गी	S	S	ए	रि	मा	S	ह
0				3								2			
प			म									सा			
ग	मं	प	ग	म	रे	सा	–	सा	–	रे	सा	.ध	–	प़	प़
अ	प	नै	बा	ल	म	को	S	ने	S	न	न	में	S	क	र
0				3								2			
सा	-	सा	-	रे	रे	सा	सा	गमप	गम	रे	सा	-	रे	सा	-
रा	S	खी	S	प	ल	क	न	मूंSS	SS	द	मूं	S	द,	का	S
0				3								2			

अन्तरा

म			प												
प	प	प	सां	–	सां	सां	-	सां	-	सां	-	सां	रें	सां	–
च	म	क	बी	S	ज	री	S	मे	S	छा	S	ब	र	से	S
0				3				x				2			
नि	नि	नि	नि									सां			
ध	ध	धा	ध	सां	–	सां	–	निसां	रे	सां	सां	थ	–	निं	प
स	दा	S	रं	गी	S	ले	S	मींS	S	म	द	सा	S	S	S
0				3								2			
ग									प						
म	रे	प	–	ध	–	प	-	मपध	मप	ग	म	सा	रे	सा	–
ब	र	से	S	मं	S	हा	S	बूंSS	SS	द	बूं		द,	का	।
0				3								2			

क्रमिक पुस्तक मालिका, भाग 4, पृष्ठ 102-103.

सदारंग कृत ख्याल, राग शंकरा - त्रिताल (विलंबित)

स्थायी

घ		घ		प				मे							
सांघ	सां(सा)	निनि	(प)	ग	प	सां	नि	प	ग	-	(प)	ग	रे	सा	-
घू	मा	लं	दि	या	s	s	s	s	s	s	s	तैं	s	डी	s
3				x				2				0			
नि़								ग				रे			
सा	रे	सा	ग	–	गरे	प	ग	प	(प)	ग	प	ग	रे	सा	नि़सा
वै	s	s	s	s	ss	s	s	मी	s	s	s	s	s	यां	ss
3				x				2				0			

अन्तरा

प								घ	सां			नि			
ग	प	सांघ	सां	सां	सां	रे	सां	सां	घ	सां	सां	सां	रें	सा	–
का	s	दs	र	कु	द	र	त	हां	बी	स	ब	ते	s	नुं	s
3								2				0			
नि	सां	सां						सां	सां			म			
सां	घ	घ	–	सां	सां	(सां)	घ	घ	घ	सां	–	प	घ	प	–
ह	इक	दी	s	अ	खि	यां	s	गु	मा	s	s	नी	s	यां	s
3				x				2				0			
ग	ग	ग		ाा								गि			
ग	ग	रे	ग	प	घ	सां	–	पपघनि	सांरें	–	सां	सां	(सा)	-	घ
स	दा	s	रं	s	ग	दी	s	ssss	ss	s	s	यां	s	s	s
3				x				2				0			

क्रतिक पुस्तक मालिका, भाग 4, पृष्ठ 230-231 ।

सदारंग कृत ख्याल, राग मियांमल्लार - एकताल (विलम्बित)[1]

स्थायी

			प							म	
प	प	प	नि̲	म	प	सां	—	—	धप	ग̲	—
मं	म	द	सा	ऽ	रं	गी	ऽ	ऽ	ल	रे	ऽ
0		3		4				0		2	
म								म			
ग	म	रे	रे	सा	-	सां	सा	ग̲	गम	रे	-
ऽ	ऽ	ब	ल	मा	ऽ	तु	भ	बि	न	में	ऽ
0		3		4				0		2	
		नि									
सा	-	सा	म	-	मरे	प	प	प	मप	प	प
का	ऽ	का	री	ऽ	बऽ	द	रि	या	ऽऽ	ने	क
0		3		4				0		2	
निध	नि̲ध	नि	प	मप	धनि	सांरे	सांनि	सां	सां	-	निसां
नाऽ	ऽऽ	ऽ	सु	हाऽ	ऽऽ	ऽऽ	ऽऽ	ऽ	वे	ऽ	ऽऽ
0		3		4				0		2	
प			प								
नि̲	प	प	नि̲	म	प						
मं	म	द	सा	ऽ	रं						
0		3		4							

1. क्रमिक पुस्तक मालिका, भाग 4, पृष्ठ 579–80

अन्तरा

रे						सां					
म	मरे	प	प	निध	निध	नि	सां	-	सां	-	सां
उ	म	ड़	घु	म	ड़	घ	न	S	आ	S	वे
x		0		2		0		3		4	
									ध	ध	
निध	निध	नि	सां	-	सां	रें	नि	सां	नि	नि	प
नै	न	न	झ		र	ल	गा	S	S	S	वे
x		0		2		0		3		4	
		म	म			म	म	रे		सा	
म	प	ग	ग	म	प	ग	ग	म	रे	रे	सा
त	र	सा		वे	स	दा		रं	गि	ले	को
x		0		2		0		3		4	
सा		मं								प	
नि	सां	गं	मं	रें	सां	नि	सां	-	प	नि	प
सु	ख	दा		ई	च	म	क		बि	च	ड
x		0		2		0		3		4	
				घ					घ	नि	
घनि	संरिं	नि	सां	नि	सां	रें	नि	सां	नि	म	प
राS	SS	वे	S	S	S	मं	म	द	सा	S	रं।
x		0		2		0		3		4	

अदारंग कृत ख्याल, राग शुद्ध कल्याण

स्थायी

.ध				रे				पप							
.प	.ध	सा	रे	ग	–	ग	–	ग	ग	–	रे	घघपमें	प	ग	रे
जा	s	को	s	दा	s	ता	s	घ	न	s	s	दीsss	s	जे	s
3				x				2				0			
नि		ग			प			प				ग			
सा	-	रे	ग	-	ग	घ	-	घ	प	ग	रे	रे	ग	रे	सा
वा	s	को	s	s	हि	म	s	त	न	s	s	दे	s	s	त
3				x				2				0			
नि		घ		प				ग				प			
सा	-	प	पं	साध	सा	सा	सा	रे	ग	·	गरे	ग	प	ग	रे
ता	s	को	अ	दा	s	रं	ग	हि	म	s	त	दी	s	ये	s
3				x				2				0			
गमप	रे	सा	-	सा	मग	प	-	प	घ	घ	-	पघसांसां	घपगरे	सासारेरे	घघसासा
वाss	s	को	s	घ	नुs	को	s	s	s	ना	s	दsss	ssss	ssss	तेsss
3				x		2					0				

अन्तरा

सा			ध												
निध	सां	(सां)	निनि	(प)	-	सांसांनिध	निध	सां	सां	सां	निसां	सां	(सां)	-	रे
क	री	s	मs	रा	s	ssss	ss	ब	द	स्तं	ss	दी	रं	s	s
								2				0			
								पध							
सां	(सां)	-	निध	प	मेग	प	प	निनि	(प)	म	ग	प	(प)	ग	रे
मे	s	s	ss	s	ss	s	स्तं	खुs	दा	s	s	बं	s	दा	s
3				X				2				0			
				नि	सा				म						
गमेप	रे	सासारे	सा	सा	मेग	प	-	-	प	घ	-	पघसांसां	घपगरे	सासारे	रेघघसा
न्याss	s	मss	त	क	रs	मे	s	s	ने	s	s	ssss	ssss	ssss	स्तं ss
3					x			2				0			

क्रमिक पुस्तक मालिका, भाग-4, पृष्ठ 74 ।

अदारंग कृत ख़याल, राग मियांमल्लार - एकताल

(विलम्बित)[1]

स्थायी

		ध		ध				ध			रे क नि
सा	निसा	नि	प,मप	नि	निध	नि	सा	नि	सा	सा	सा
री	SS	S	म,SS	ना	SS	म	ते	S	S	रो	तु
3		4		x		0		2		0	
				सा	म	म					
-	सा	रे	सा	प	ग	ग	म	रे	-	सा,निसा	रे
S	सा	हे	ब	स	त्ता	S	S	S	S	र,SS	क
3		4		X			0		2	0	

अन्तरा

							नि		ध		
मप	प,निध	निध	नि	सां	-	सां	सां	रें	सां	निध	निध
दुख	द,लि		द्र	दू		र	की		जै	सु	ख
3		4		x		0		2		0	
निध	नि	सां	सां	रे	सां	(सा)	ध	नि	प	म	प
SS	दै	ह	हो	स	ब	न	को	S	S	अ	दा
3		4		x		0		2		0	
	प	ध		म	म			सा			
मप	नि	नि	प	ग	ग	म	रे	रे	सा	म	प
SS	रं	S	ग	बि	न	ति	क	र	त	सु	न
3		4		x		0		2		0	
मप	निध	सां	सां	प	ग	ग	म	रे	-	सा,निसा,रे	
	लें		हो	स	त्ता	S	S	S	S	र,SS	क।
3		4		x		0		3			0

1. क्रमिक पुस्तक मालिका, भाग 4, पृष्ठ 582-83

मनरंग कृत ख्याल, राग शुद्ध कल्याण
देशकार आड़ा चौताल (विलंम्बित)

स्थायी

				सा					ग				
ग	रे	सा,रेध	सा	प	ग	प	प	-	प	प	प	ध	-
ज	ब	प,ऽऽ	र	दे	ऽ	ऽ	स	ऽ	ग	व	न	ऽ	ऽ
4		0		x		2		0		3		0	
ग				ग	प					सां		ध	
प	ध	प	ग	प	ग	-	प	-	ध	ध	सां	-	सां
की	ऽ	नो	ऽ	त	ब	ऽ	ते	ऽ	ऽ	त	न	ऽ	म
4		0		x		2		0		3		0	
				ध			ग			ध			रे
ध	-	प	-	ग	प	-	प	ध	-	पधसांसा	धपगरे	सा	धसा
ऽ	ऽ	यो	ऽ	सु	ऽ	ऽ	ख	ऽ	ऽ	माऽऽऽ	ऽऽऽऽ	ई	ऽऽ
4		0		x		2		0		3		0	

अन्तरा

										ध	सां		
प	ध	सां	सां	सां	-	-	सां	-	सां	सां	ध	-	सां
म	न	रं	ग	पी	ऽ	ऽ	त	ऽ	म	क	ब	ऽ	ध
4		0		x		2		0		3		0	
		ध				सां		ग	प				
सां	रें	सां	रें	-	सां	ध	प	प	ग	-	प	ध	-
र		आ	ऽ	ऽ	वें	गे	ऽ	जि	या	ऽ	में	ऽ	ऽ
4		0		x		2		0	3		0		
ध				ध									रे
सां	-	ध	प	ग	प	-	प	ध	-	पधसांसां	धपगरे	सासारेंरे	धसा
ऊ	ऽ	ठ	त	हू	ऽ	ऽ	क	ऽ	ऽ	माऽऽऽ	ऽऽऽऽ	ऽऽऽऽ	इऽऽ
4		0		x		2		0		3		0	

क्रमिक पुस्तक मालिका, भाग 4, पृष्ठ 260–261.

CHAPTER VIII

SUR-SRINGAR AND SUR-BAHAR EVOLUTION AND CONTRIBUTIONS BY SENIA'S

Sur-Sringar was invented by Jafar Khan a descendant of Tansen, in the early part of the nineteenth Century and set it in vogue. Once he and his cousin Nirmal Shah had to demonstrate their skill on the Rabab and Veena respectively at the court of Banaras. After Nirmal Shah had done so, it was Jafar Khan's turn to play. It being the rainy season he found his instrument (covered with hide and played mostly on catgut), being damp, would not emit good tones. His position became awkward in the *soiree* as Nirmal Shah and he had always been competitors for leadership in the world of Indian music.

He took a month's time from the Maharaja of Banaras Raja Udit Narayan Singh, promising to demonstrate his art at the end of it. During this period he came and stayed with an instrument-maker of the city and evolved a new instrument on the basis of the Rabab. It was Rabab-like in shape but instead of the skin covering the lower portion a thin metal plate covered the whole upper surface and instead of the silk chord and catgut used in the Ràbab, steel and brass wires were put into use. This change breathed a new life into the instrument. Compared to the Veena the tones of the new instrument were louder but sweeter and better than the Rabab which was harsh. Both techniques of Veena and Rabab playing could be used on this instrument not only successfully but to the best advantage of the player.[1]

1. Goswami O, The story of Indian Music, pp. 302-303.

All the phrases of *Alap* can be produced on this instrument. it is quite suitable for the *Govarhar* and *Dagar Vani's.* [1]

Raja Surinder Mohan Tagore says that the instrument is made by combining the features of *Mahati Veena, Kachhapi Veena* and *Rudra Veena* into one. The gourd resonator, the *Dhvani-Pattak (Tabli)* are all like those of *Kachhapi Veena*, the finger board *(Dand)* is like that of *Rudra Veena* or Rabab, and the upper gourd is like that of *Mahati Veena*. The Rabab's finger board is only of wood, whereas the Sur-Sringars finger *board* of wood is covered on the upper portion by a metal plate called Patri.[2] Sur-Sringar has no frets. Like Sitar, it has a bridge-*Sawari*. The Strings which are mounted on the bridge, pass over the plate and are tied on the other end to wooden *"Khunti's"*. Another gourd is attached to the top for the purpose of resonance. Unlike Rabab, this instrument contains six metal strings, three of steel and three of brass.

The Sur-Sringar is held like Rabab. It is placed on the left shoulder. The index and the middle fingers of the left hand glide over the strings. An iron plectrum held by the index and the middle fingers of the right hand plays on the strings like Rabab. the Sur-Sringars range goes upto two and half octaves.

The Sur-Sringar has a very soft sound which does not stay long.

Inspite of its association with Tansen and his descendants, the Rabab suffered from certain initial handicaps. As has already been said, it did not lend itself to *Vilambit Alap*, During the rains its sound deteriorated, so much so that sometimes even the notes could not be easily distinguished. Hence the instrument could never gain popularity. The Sur-Sringar, because of its elongated size, steel strings and metal plate in place of catguts and wooden finger board, was a distinct improvement over the Rabab with regard to both the tonal quality and performances. It may very well appear that the Sur-Sringar combines in itself some of the structural features of the sitar and the sarode. The finger board with its steel plate

1. Personal Communications with Shri Birendra Kishore Roy Chaudhuri.
2. Raja Surinder Mohan Tagore, 'History of Indian Music', p. 33.

has been taken from the sarode and the lower portion, the gourd, the resonator and the Jawari appear to have been borrowed from the Sitar.

CONTRIBUTIONS OF SENIA'S

In Senia Gharana there were some famous exponents of Sur-Sringar. Among them Jafar Khan, Pyar Khan and Bahadur Hussain Khan were the great exponents of Sur-Sringar.

After the invention of Sur-Sringar by Jafar Khan, Pyar Khan his next brother specialised in this instrument and added some fascinating ornamentations in the style of its display. Pyar Khan and Umrao Khan gave many friendly duets of instrumental music Sur-Sringar and Veena in Varanasi.

Bahadur Hussain Khan was adopted son of Pyar Khan. he concentrated more on instrumental music. He first used to play on the Sur-Sringar and then on the Veena. He had such a charming style of play that people used to say that his fingers were made of diamonds. Not only the lovers of classical music, but even uninitiated laymen were overwhelmed with rapturous joy by the sound of his instrumental displays. He introduced many new *Alankars* in the instrumental music and variations of *Jhala* or *Jhankar* which are unequalled even up to now by any instrumentalist of India playing Sitar or Sarode.

Birendra Kishore Roy Chaudhuri states that the Rampur Gharana of music is founded by Bahadur Hussain Khan and Amir Khan, his son-in-law. They both were characterised by some special charms in the use of *Alap*, Dhrupad, Dhamar and the Instrumental Music which were not found anywhere in India. Both of these great musicians gave all their theoretical and practical knowledge to Nawab Haider Ali Khan a brother of the then ruling Nawab of Rampur.

During the time of Haider Ali Khan, Rampur state had a galaxy of musicians. All of them became disciples of Bahadur Hussain and Amir Khan. Although they belonged to other Gharanas before they came to Rampur, they changed their old style and were influenced by the styles of their masters and thus became identified with the Rampur Gharana. Bahadur Hussain Khan composed many *Taranas* and *Lakshan Geets.* One of them is given at the last of this Chapter.

In Senia Gharanas Ali Muhammad Khan, son of Basat Khan was another accomplished Sur-Sringar player. According to Birendra Kishore Roy Chaudhuri, Ali Muhammad Khan was a very liberal minded musicians and used to play on his Sur-Sringar before his disciples without any reservation.[1] He had profound knowledge of Ragas and could develop any Raga for hours without any repetitions of the *Tanas.* He trained up many musicians in Sur-Sringar. Syed Mir Nasir Khan of Jullundhar was his most accomplished disciple in Sur-Sringar.[2] He also imparted lessons of Vocal Music of Dhrupada and Instrumental Music on Veena and Sur-Sringar to Wazir Khan of Rampur.

Wazir Khan got his initial training from his father in Been and in Sur-Sringar from Bahadur Hussain Khan. He was both a melodious Vocalist and a great instrumentalist. He built up the musical career of many outstanding musicians.

Dabir Khan the grandson of Wazir Khan was a great Vocalist as well as great instrumentalist. He was an accomplished Sur-Sringar player.

Another reputed Sur-Sringar player of Senia Gharana was Salamat Hussain Khan of Rampur. He had his training in the instrument from his maternal grand father, Asad Ali Khan. Later, he had further training in Sur-Sringar, Dhrupada and Veena from the Nawab Chhaman Saheb of Rampur and the last Senia, Mohammad Ali Khan.

Kumar Birendra Kishore Roy Chaudhuri, who learnt from Muhammad Ali Khan, the last Senia exponent at the Rampur Court, was also a distinguished Sur-Sringar player.

In Senia Gharana the another Sur-Sringar player was Saukat Ali Khan. He was the adopted son of Muhammad Ali Khan.

Ustad Allauddin Khan and Ustad Hafiz Ali Khan both

---

1. Roy Chaudhuri Birendra Kishore , 'Indian Music & Mian Tansen', p. 23.
2. Ibid.

had their training in Sur-Sringar under the late Ustad Wazir Khan and Dabir Khan of Rampur and were highly proficient in the art of playing the instrument.

Accoding to Ustad Ali Akbar Khan and Prof. Radhika Mohan Moitra, Sarode players previously used to play *alap* on the Sur-Sringar and then wind up their recital by playing *Gat Toda* on the Sarode.

In the technique of playing by Senia's, the instrument follows all the principles of the *Veena Ang Alap* including *Ladi Lad Guthavo, Tar-Paran Jhala* etc.

According to Shri Birendra Kishore Roy Chaudhuri, the melodic effect of the Sur-Sringar is extraordinary and outshines even that of the Veena in *Vilambit Alap.* Prof. Radhika Mohan Moitra states that Sur-Sringar and Sur-Bahar are not used for playing *Gat-Toda.* This may be one reason why these two instruments do not enjoy the same popularity which they once used to do.

Some talented artists of the present generation have been experimenting with the Sitar and Sarode with a view of improving their tonal quality and the range of *Meend* and *Sut.* Ustad Ali Akbar Khan and Prof. Radhika Mohan Moitra have proved that with slight modification these instruments can lend themselves equally to *Alap* and *Gat Toda.*

SUR-BAHAR

The Sur-Bahar is a comparatively modern instrument. Shri Birendra Kishore Roy Chaudhuri, in his book "Hindusthaner Sangite Tansener Sthan", states that Umrao Khan of Senia Gharana made a big Sitar and named it as Sur-Bahar, which he taught to his pupil Kutubuddaullah and Ghulam Mohammad Khan; its mode of display.[1]

Raja Surinder Mohan Tagore mentions that Ghulam Mohammad Khan, a student of Pyar Khan of Senia Gharana, introduced this instrument[2], Ghulam Mohammad Khan was a *Beenkar* at the court of the Nawab of Lucknow. Possibly Ghulam Mohammad Khan might have popularised the Sur-Bahar and his son Sajjad Muhammad

1. Roy Chaudhuri Birendra Kishore, "Hindusthaner Sangite Tansener Sthan", p. 100.
2. Tagore Surinder Mohan, "Yantra Kosh", p. 32.

Khan made further improvement on it.

The instrument was specially meant for *Alap* The *Tarab* and *Chikkaris* were applied to the instrument and subsequently, these strings were introduced as an addition to the Sitar.[1]

Among the living musician in Senia Gharana, only Ustad Mushtaq Ali Khan plays Sur-Bahar in accordance with the Veena technique. But it has become much less popular these days.

According to Ustad Mushtaq Ali Khan the Sur-Bahar is meant only for *Alap*, and the *Alap*. should be executed like Veena's thirteen Alap divisions.[2]

Playing of *Gats* like *Maseetkhani* and *Razakhani* is strictly prohibited in Sur-Bahar. The exposition of *Thumri-Ang Ragas* are also not meant for Sur-Bahar and hence, the use of *Khatkas* and *Murkis* is also prohibited. He further states that Sur-Bahar is played in the technique of Veena with the help of three Mizrabs. Shrimati Annapurna Devi, wife of Pandit Ravi Shankar, also plays Sur-Bahar in this technique.

Shri Bimal Kant Roy Chaudhuri and Jiten Sen also had their training in Sur-Bahar and were playing Sur-Bahar in *Veena Ang*. A Sitar player generally used to execute *Alap* on Sur-Bahar and played *Gat Todas* on the Sitar. Due to its structural peculiarity, the Sur-Bahar lends itself more to the graces of *Dagar* and *Gobarhar Vani* than other recognised *Vanis*.

Ustad Ashiq Ali Khan combined Dhrupad and Khayal elements in Sur-Bahar.[3] Among the few Sur-Bahar players of the country today, is Imrat Hussain Khan, the youngest son of Ustad Inayat Khan. He plays Sur-Bahar in Sitar technique. He uses all the *Alankars* like *Khatka, Murki* etc., of Khayal in his Sur-Bahar. This style does not at all conform to the rules of the Veena.

Consequently, *Tanas* and *Pallas* came into use in Sur-Bahar too, and the style became different from the Orthodox Sur-Bahar technique which followed the *Veena Ang* strictly.

1. Personal Communications with Ustad Mushtaq Ali Khan.
2. Ibid.
3. Choudhuri shri Bimal Kant, 'Bhartiya Sangeet Kosh'.

CHAPTER IX

SITAR, ITS EVOLUTION, CONTRIBUTIONS,TECHNIQUE OF PLAYING AND THE COMPOSITIONS BY SENIA'S

The Veena appears to have been prototype of all the Indian string instruments. Most probably the Kachhapi Veena and Tritantri Veena resembles the modern Sitar and the Sitar was progressive development of these two.[1]

Despite its obvious relationship with the Veena the origin of the sitar remains shrouded in mystery. Most interesting however, is the etymology of the word Sitar.

In Medieval France we find a kind of lute called Sitahray[2] In 16th and 17th Century in medieval France a Persian Guitar was known as Sitahray. In England 16th and 17th Century, a Persian Guitar was known as Stern and was extremely popular.

The ancient Greeks themselves pronounced Sitarah as Kitarah.[3] The Arabs had a similar instrument named the Hitar, which eventually found its way to Spain, where it became known as the Guitarah.

In the Anand Raj Hindi dictionary and 'Sharfana" the Persian dictionary, the word Sitarah or Seh-Tar occurs.

नाम साजें अस्त दो सिताराह

गोयंदश वो नीज़ सेहतार[4]

---

1. A Documentary Film on the Evolution of Sitar by Pandit Ravi Shankar.
2. Ibid.
3. Ibid.
4. Loghat Nama - Encyclopaedia, Series No. 83, p. 296

Again in the Burhan dictionary the Sitarah and the Tanburah are considered to be the same instruments.

तम्बूराह वो साजे रा गोयदं

कि सेहतार दाश्ताह बाबद

The Arabian Guitar today is still known as Guitar and a five stringed Nayar called the Kiscar.[1]

Modern Greece have a beautiful similar instrument named Zither a direct descendant of the ancient Sitarah.

In the Persian Encyclopaedia "Loghatnama" we find reference to Seh-Tar which is popular in the Kanuni language.

दर ज़बान कानूनी नीज़ सेहतार [2]

If the word Seh-Tar is analysed, we get the following meanings.

सेह+तार+ हे (निस्बत) दाराह

सेह सीम रक

निस्बत	means	relations
सेह	means	Three
सीम	means	Strings of an Instrument
रक	means	Changing of the neck
दाराह	means	holding fast

Traditionally its invention is ascribed to the renowned Poet, Musician, Historian Hazrat Amir Khusroo of the 13th and early 14th Century. But in Amir Khusroo's works, the name Sitar does not appear in the list of other musical stringed instruments in his two Masnavis :

1. "Ishaqia" (Love episodes of Khizr Khan and Devel Devi).
2. Qiran-us-Saddain (Meeting of the two propitious stars)

We get the descriptive terminology for musical modes, notes and instruments. The musical instruments were called Saz or Alat by Amir Khusroo.[3] Among the strings there were

1. Documentary Film on Evolution of Sitar by Pandit Ravi Shankar.
2. Loghatnama - Encyclopedia Series No. 83 p. 293.
3. The Article on Amir Khusroo and Music by Prof. S.H. Askari, p. 23.

Chang, Rabab, Tanbur, Barbat, Rud and *Ud.*[1] But the word Sitar as a musical instrument was not mentioned in Amir Khusroo's works.

Mohammad Wahid Mirza holds that in Amir Khusroo's writings pages are full of descriptions of various musical instruments, unfortunately he is unable to trace anywhere the name of Sitar. He also adds that the only instrument peculiar to India, probably a new invention, would seem to be the *Ajab Rud* which does not appear to resemble the Sitar at all.[2]

Even Abul Fazal does not mention it in the list of instruments but mentions the name of *Yantra* an instrument one yard in length and made of wood and hollow from inside, to which pumpkin gourds were attached at both ends and had five steel strings.[3] The word *Yantra* was known at one time *Tritantri Veena.*

Kallinatha in his commentary on Sangeet Ratnakar writes :-

"त्रिन्तकैव लोके यन्त्र शब्दे नोच्यते"

Abul Fazal says the another instrument called Been was like Yantra and contained three strings. Abul Fazal in describing this writes :-

"जन्त्र आसा लेकिन सेहतार द्वारद" [4]

Probably from the Seh-Tar the word Sitar is derived. The Sitar which resembles the Persian Tambura or Ud in shape and the Indian Veena in principle, is itself a fusion and an epitome of the Indo-Persian Culture and Civilization.

Thus it is likely that the modern Guitar, Guitern, Seh-Tar, Sitarah and Sitar are all cousins tracing the genealogy back to one mother instrument which unfortunately has been obscured by the clouds of history.

The next version is that the sitar was introduced by the Khusroo Khan, the younger brother of Niyamat Khan Sadarang. After that Masit Khan, the 7th descendant of Mian Tansen originated the Sitar with extra strings.[5]

---

1. The Article on Amir Khusroo and Music by Prof. S.H. Askari, p. 23.
2. The life and works of Amir Khusroo by Mohammad Wahid Mirza.
3. Abul Fazal, Ain-I-Akbari, Vol. III, pp. 288-289.
4. Ibid., pp. 110-111.
5. Acharya Sudarhan, Sangeet Sudarshan, p. 17.

CONTRIBUTION OF SENIA'S

The name Sitar has been mentioned for the first time in the text book of Hakim Karam Imam's "Madunul Mausiqui" written during the time of Wazed Ali Shah, 1855 A.D. The Sitar of this time had one gourd, fourteen frets and three strings.[1]

Gradually the developments in Sitar were brought about by the Senias'. Khusroo Khan introduced the Sitar, besides that one of his speciality was that he could play this particular type of instrument Sitar for a very long duration in different ways. On Sitar he could play *Ragas* and *Raginis.* He had also innovated a number of New *Ragas* and *Raginis.*

Another Sitar maestro was Feroj Khan, the son of Khusroo Khan and father of Masit Khan or Sen and was married to the daughter of Sadarang. Although he was a Dhrupad singer but he was the master of the Sitar also.

Feroj Khan taught Sitar to his son Masit Khan. *Maseet Khani Baj* of *Vilambit* which is also known as *Delhi Ka Baj* is famous after his name as he invented it and used it first. During his time no *Jod* used to be played on Sitar only *Gat* and *Toda* used to be played. The Sitar in its present shape and form owes much to the pioneering work done by Masit Khan.

A strict follower of Dhrupada tradition, Masit Khan composed his *Gats* in the four principle movements of the *Dhrupada Sthayi, Antara, Sanchari* and *Abhog.*. Masit Khan laid great emphasis on the importance of *bols* played with right hand which were crystallised into a definite shape and the *bols* were standarised. These *Gats* having a positive form with *Asthai* and *Antara* fully rendered were followed by *Todas* in *Vilambit Laya*. The *Todas* were composed on the basis of *Parans* of *Pakhawaj* or *Tabla*. Masit Khan taught Sitar to his sisters son Dulhe Khan. Sukh Sen, Nur Sen, and Bahadur Sen were his own sons. Descendants of Masit Khan composed many *Gats* for the Sitar which can even now be heard from *Ustads* following strict traditions

1. Hakim Muhammad Karam Imam, 'Madunul Mausiqui, p. 157.

of *Maseetkhani Baj* through simple and shorn of all embellishments, were rich in tone and colour.

Bahadur Sen, the son of Masit Khan was a good Sitar player and was famous for composing *Gats* and *Todas* in Sitar.

Dulhe Khan was son of Feroj Khan (Adarang). He was the master of Been and Dhrupada and had his training in Sitar from his maternal uncle Masit Khan. He remained for some time with the Naresh of Gwalior. Dulhe Khan had one daughter, who was married to Rahim Sen.

Rahim Sen was from the line of Bilas Khan of Senia Gharana.[1] His father's name was Sukh Sen. Many authors report that Rahim Sen was the son of Masit Khan,[2] but Sudarshan Acharya states that Masit Khan was a descendant of Misri Singh the son-in-law of Tansen, while as Rahim Sen was descendant of Bilas Khan.

Sudarshan Acharya further states that Rahim Sen was first from Bilas Khan's line who played Sitar. Before Rahim Sen, the Sitar was played by the daughters line of Tansen. He is credited with having brought Sitar to the level of Veena which was most played and liked instrument of that time. Rahim Sen along with his son, Amrit Sen introduced Veena, Dhrupada and Khayal all the three into the Sitar and used to play first *Jod* and then *Gat Toda* and then *Jhala*. In it *Jod* is from Veena, *Alap, Gat* and *Toda* from Dhrupada and *Asthai* from Khayal.

Amrit Sen was elder son of Rahim Sen. He was a very good Dhrupad singer in *Goudhar Vani,* although he never used to sing in the public since his father had advised him not to sing or play except play Sitar in public. By the age of ten years Amrit Sen used to play Sitar along with his father Rahim Sen on stages and by the age of thirteen years, he started giving solo performances in Sitar. He named his Sitar as *Mani Ram.*[3]

It is believed that Rahim Sen and Amrit Sen played Sitar so beautifully that their melody in playing resulted into the death of other instruments and Dhrupada in their family.

1. Sudarshan Acharya, 'Sangeet Sudarshan', p. 27.
2. Acharya Brahaspati, 'Musalman Aur Bhartiya Sangeet', p. 38.
3. Acharya Sudarshan, 'Sangeet Sudarshan', p.16.

They both were credited with introduction of greater use of *Meend.* They also introduced the element of *Layakari* in *Maseet Khani Baj. Fiqure Bandi*, which was a characteristic Khayal technique, was introduced by them. It consisted of a small *Toda* employing a variety of *Bajs* played with great gusto at the close of the *Gat.* According to Sudarshan Acharya fast *Todas* played in a zig zag pattern in the *Gat* technique of Sitar is called *Fiqure Bandi* which was derived from Khayal and Qawwali.[1] They both were the first poineers incorporating the *Been Ang* with special emphasis to *Alap* and *Jod* on Sitar, which was to be followed by *Gat Toda.*

Rahim Sen, Amrit Sen both were generally acknowledged the greatest among the Senia's. They invariably avoided the use of single note *tanas* which are so popular with the Sitar players today. They excelled in the use of *Baj Tanas*, which gave them full scope for displaying mastery of the right hand technique. In *bol Tanas* the mizrab plays an important part. They were also great masters of playing the *Kulfidar Tanas* on the Sitar. They also used to perform on the sitar some angas like *Ladi Lad, Lapet* and *Lad Guthav* of the *Veena* before concluding their recital. It was Rahim Sen who emerged as the interpreter of the new techniques which was further popularised by Amrit Sen. Amrit Sen has advocated the use of seventeen frets in the sitar.

Sudarshan Acharya in his book Sangeet Sudarshan gave the following arrangement of frets as introduced by Amrit Sen :-

मे प ध॒ ध नि॒ सा रे ग म

मे प ध नि सं रें गं मं

Amrit Sen's Sitar had six strings and no *Chikari.* We find mention of the *Chikari* in 'Nadvinode' written earlier not used by Senias' who played only *Gat* and *Toda.* The tuning system was introduced by Amrit Sen and is as follows :-

The main string was tuned to *Madhyama* followed by two to *Shadjas* and two to *Panchamas* and some Senia's also

1. Acharya Sudarshan, 'Sangeet Sudarshan', p 27.

used as *Kharaj*. Almost all Sitar players have switched over to the use of nineteen frets. Only a few perhaps only one of the orthodox school still use seventeen frets. For an additional Chikari Strings, the present day Sitar players follow more or less the same system of tuning as was prevalent during Amrit Sen's time.

Haider Khan or Baksh, son of Dulhe Khan and maternal uncle of Amrit Sen, was a Dhrupada singer and had a good knowledge of music. Besides Dhrupada, he had a good knowledge of Sitar and Beena and gave training in music to many of his students. At his death Amrit Sen said. "The Music School of our home has died today". Haider Baksh had five sons they were Wazir Khan, Almu Khan, Mamu Khan, Salawat Khan and Alawat Khan. All these brothers learnt from Amrit Sen and mostly lived with him. All of them had great collections of Drupadas and were master exponents of Sitar.

Amrit Sen had two brothers whose names were Niyamat Sen and Lal Sen. Niyamat Sen, who learnt Sitar from Amrit Sen, was very good in Sitar and had a delicate and sweet hand for Sitar, but died at a very young age. Lal Sen developed certain defects in his hands and could not persue Sitar subsequently.

Amrit Sen had no son. He adopted Nihal Khan or Sen, the son of Wazir Khan who took his place in the Court of Ram singh of Jaipur. He also learnt Sitar from Amrit Sen. Nihal Sen's sons, Fida Hussain and Fazal Hussain, were also noted Sitar players of Senia Gharana. It was Nihal Sen who introduced the *Tarab* strings in the Sitar.[1]

The another son of Wazir Khan was Amir Khan born at Jhanjar and had his education in Sitar from Amrit Sen and also from his maternal grandfather Rahim Sen. Amir Khan was a good Sitar player and had a deep knowledge of music also. Amir Khan initially remained more with Alwar Naresh than with Ram Singh of Jaipur, than in Gwalior with Jiya Ji Maharaj, and was Guru of Madhav Rao Maharaj, who was son of Jiya Ji. Amir Khan passed away in 1915. According to Late Radhika Mohan Moitra

---

1. Dr. Sharmistha Sen's Thesis based on String Instruments.

Ustad Barkatullah Khan was initially a Pakhawaj player but became disciple of Amir Khan and learned Sitar from him. Although he was a Pakhawaj player but he acquired a mastery over the sitar and became the most brilliant Sitar player of his time in Senia Gharana. He was a Court Musician in Patiala and Mysore. His disc record of a *Gat* in *Bhubkalyani* gives us some idea of the authentic Senia *Baj*. The descendants of Amrit Sen prefered to play in pair rather than solo. While one kept the rhythm of the Gat, the other played a variety of *Toda* and vice versa.

Barkatullah Khan taught sitar to Ustad Ashiq Ali Khan, who was an accomplished Sitar player of his time. He was a Sur-Bahar player also. He was famous for Alap and Jod Ang technique in both Sitar and Sur-Bahar.

After the death of these musicians, the Senia Baj began to loose its popularity. It might be due to the fact that no good sitar players among the Senia's could take the place of the great masters. It might be that people were also getting tired of the strict traditional Sitarists and they wanted something new. The second reason could be that the emergence of Khayal as an established Vocal form, made an impact on the muscians as well as the listners and a new taste developed. This brought a revolutionary change in the style of Sitar playing both in *Maseetkhani Baj* and in *Razakhani style*.

In Karam Imam's 'Madunul Mausiqui', we find Ghulam Raza playing in *Razakhani* style to please the noble men of Lucknow.[1] Ghulam Raza and his sons were noted players on Sitar and the style of their execution has been followed in parts of the country.[2]

Hakim Karam Imam for the style of Ghulam Raza, writes, "I have not heard any other person playing it so well except Ghulam Raza." The *Razakhani* style is also referred to as Purab Ka Baj, apparantly because it was more popular in the Eastern part of the country. This style follows no tradition and is unsystematic. Its Gats in Teental are composed in the style of *thumri Ragini* and *Dhun* etc.

The *Razakhani* Gats were also set to *Teental* but in Dr[illegible]

1. Translation of Madunul Mausiqui by Govind Vidyarathi, p. 23.
2. Tagore Surinder Mohan, 'Universal History of India'. p. 76.

Laya. It necessitated both the left and the right hands to move faster. The *Razakhani Gat* was mainly based on *bols.*

Senia's were playing both the *Gats* in *Teental* and the *bols* of these *Gats* were distinct. The *bols* of this *Gat* can be used in combination, for instance, Da, Ra, Da may be produced as single bol *Darda,* but such a combination of *Bols* does not effect its rhythmic value which consists of three *matras* or units of time.

A famous disciple of Wazir Khan and an extraordinary teacher and performer was Ustad Allauddin Khan of Maihar. He was one of the sons of a quite well to do peasant family in Bengal. He made tremendous contributions to the world of music especially in the instrumental field. Above all he is responsible for enlarging the scope and range of possibilities open to an instrumentalist. He was taught by many masters.

Pandit Ravi Shankar states, "Ustad Ji played the violin with his left hand", and once gave an impressive performance on the Sarod and on the Violin, and then was asked if he could handle any other instruments. The Nawab was quite amused when Khan Saheb replying, boasted that he could play any instrument available in the palace. So, all the instruments were brought out and, to the astonishment of everyone present, he did, just that, one by one he played them all and quite deftly too. Once Nawab asked him if he had any other talents, Khan Saheb said that he could write anything played or sung. The Nawab was overwhelmed when Khan Saheb did this easily on the first attempt. The Nawab then sang a very difficult *Gamak Tan,* a complicated embellishment in a Phrase. Fortunately, Allauddin Khan detected that the Nawab was becoming a little annoyed at the thought that such a young man might know more than he, so he meekly replied that such a *Tan* would be difficult to write down. The Nawab was so pleased at this that, in a benevolent mood, he sent for Ustad Wazir Khan and recommended Ustad Allauddin to him as a deserving student. The Nawab himself called for a large silver tray full of Gold sovereigns sweets, material for new clothing and a ring. All these were given to Wazir Khan on behalf of the disciple and the binding ceremony between Wazir Khan as Guru and Allauddin Khan *shishya* took place on the spot.

Rameshwar Pathak from Tansen's Gharana was the another Sitar maestro. He learnt a variety of styles of singing and playing and acquired a good many instrumental techniques. He is corporated in his playing some of the characteristcs of diverse Vocal styles and of the playing styles associated with a number of different instruments. He taught Sitar to his sons and disciples.

Only Ustad Mushtaq Ali Khan of Banaras from Senia Gharana is among the living Sitar player. He was born on 26th June, 1911 in Varanasi. He received President's Award in 1968. He learnt Sitar from his father Ustad Ashiq Ali Khan, a disciple of Ustad Barkatullah Khan and kept up the Senia tradition. He is one of the very few Sitar players of the day whose *Maseet Khani Baj* gives us some idea of the true Senia style. He is a firm believer of the rules of the orthodox Schools of Sitar technique and maintains the purity of the tradition. He is famous for *Alap* and *Jod Ang* techniques in both Sitar and Sur-Bahar. *Zamzama* and *Sut* is shown by him with great clarity.

Ustad Mushtaq Ali Khan's Sitar has seventeen frets. He had a very methodical and systematic approach towards ragas and as such his rendering of the *ragas* is pure and rigid and is devoid of environmental or modernistic influences.

Following the Senia tradition, Ustad Mushtaq Ali Khan first displays the full *Gats* and then eleborates the *Gat* in different ways of *Gatkari* or *Gat Bahlav*. Then he proceeds to *Fiqras* and *Upaj Todas* and *Kulfidar Tanas* without any *teehais*. Previously, *Maseet Khani Gats* s were improvised without *teehais* by the Senias' of Jaipur. Now-a-days it has become an almost indispensable practice to use *teehais* in both the *Gats*. The *Gats*. in Sitar by Senia's were always rendered in *Teen Tala*, because this is the only *Tala* which covers all the *bols* of both the *Gats*.

Ustad Mushtaq Ali Khan says that the Senias' had a peculiar characteristic feature known as *Dhadda Vani* or *Rasal Vani* in their style which was very appealing.[1] He got his lessons in Razakhani Gats also from Ustad Amir Khan

1. Personal Communications with Ustad Mushtaq Ali Khan of Senia Gharana.

Sarod Nawaz of Calcutta. According to Ustad Mushtaq Ali Khan the word *Manjha* in the Maseet Khani is taken from *Sozkhani* Sangeet where the names like *Matla Manjha* and *Teep* are present. The word *Manjha* actually means the middle part but is not played by him.

According to Prof. D.T. Joshi, compositions set to other Talas could not feature the correct *bols* to the two traditional *Bajs* (styles). Ustad Mushtaq Ali Khan also believes in the precision of the raga and as such, is very particular in rendering the *ragas* in *Dhrupad Ang.* He says all the Senias' music is systematically rendered in Veena technique and *Alap* akin to Dhrupad.

According to Ustad Mushtaq Ali Khan, the *Alap* portion contains broadly the following four divisions, played successively :-

1. *Vilambit* : Which contains four parts, such as *Sthai, Antara, Sanchari* and *Abhog.*
2. *Madh* : He introduced *Jod* in *Alap.* It is called *Madh.* The tempo is bit faster than that of *Vilambit.* Varieties of Sitar techniques producing *Gamakas* and *Sutas* etc. are very well displayed in *Madh.*
3. *Drut* : After displaying various combinations of notes in *Madh,* short phrases of notes in *todas* in a quicker tempo, are played followed by big pharases of notes in *tanas,* and this is known as *Drut.* The fourth one is *Jhalla* in *Alap.* At the end of this Chapter some of his compositions are given.

Among the great Sitar player of today in Senia gharana is the well known Sitar maestro, Pandit Ravi Shankar. He is a creative artist who has considerably enriched the Sitar by introducing the techniques of other string instruments.

He has introduced many South Indian ragas to Hindustani North Indian Music. A variety of *Krintans* or cut notes is a speciality in Pandit Ravi Shankar's music. He also plays in *Talas* other that *Trital. Alap* is his forte. In his music the other speciality is that he uses the strings of *Kharaj* and *Panchama* for the elaboration of *Alap-Vistara.* It is a measure of his catholicity and eclectic approach to music that we find glimpses of Karnataka technique in his Sitar, particularly in the field of *Tala*. His concert Tours abroad have made the Sitar a very popular instrument all over the world.

Pandit Ravi Shankar has replaced one *Jod String* with a *Pa* of the extreme *Kharaj*. This system which was in vogue, even when *Nad-Vinoda* was written, has evidently been popularised by Pandit Ravi Shankar now. By doing so, he has sought to impart a greater depth of feeling and at the same time, has increased the range well high to four octaves in the Alap stage. Previously *Gat Toda* was played on the Sitar and *Alap* on the Sur-Bahar. But Pandit Ravi Shankar, under the training of Ustad Allauddin Khan, however, played both *Alap* and *Gat Toda* on the Sitar. At the end of this Chapter some of his compositions are given.

The next line of musicians who follow strictly the Senia technique in Sitar is Prof. Debu Chaudhuri, born in 1935 in Calcutta. He initially received his early training from the late Panchu Gopal Dutta and later from Ustad Mushtaq Ali Khan of Senia Gharana. He has followed the path of truth and honesty in music and has strictly adhered to Senia techniques of playing Sitar. His styles are marked by a rare aesthetics sense, rhythm and unusual grace. He has also created two new ragas which are raga *Bisweswari* and *Palas-Sarang*, which have been acclaimed as the creation of a genious. He is Prof. of Music in the Faculty of Music & Fine Arts, University of Delhi and has written a book titled "Sitar and Its Technique" which has been received very well in all part of the world. Besides being a musician of pure Senia tradition, an academician, an author and a teacher, a combination very rare in India. Above all this, he is a top ranking artiste well known for his absorbing performances. At the end of this chapter some of his compositions are given.

Another noted Sitar player of today in Senia Gharana is Shri Nikhil Banerjee. He is a student of Ustad Allauddin Khan and Ali Akbar Khan. In his music which is full of aesthetic appeal, one finds a beautiful blend of the technique of Sarode and Sitar. At the end of this Chapter, I am giving few composition of old master musicians.

Raga 'Bhairavi' in Teen Tal by Senia's

स्थाई

प	प	प	गग	स	गम	गमपध	पम
						म	
गरेग	सरे	स	पध	प	मप	ग	म

मंझा

—	—	—	गग	रे	सस	नि	स
ध	निनि	सरेग	—	स	गम	गमपध	पम
गरेग	सरे	स	पध				

अन्तरा

—	—	—	गग	ग	मम	ध	नि
सं	सं	सं	गंगं	रे	संसं	नि	सं
ध	निनि	ध	प	स	गम	गमपध	पम
गरेग	सरे	स	—				

Raag Yaman in Teen Tal
By
Pyar Khan of Senia Gharana

ग	—ग	रे	नि	—नि	रे	ग	—ग
डा	डर	डा	डा	डरा	डा	डा	डर
रे	नि़	—	ग	रे	नि़	—नि	रे
डा	डा	—	डा	रा	डा	डर	डा
ग	—	ग	रे	ग	म॑म॑	प	ध
डा	—	डा	रा	डा	डिर	डा	रा
प	म॑म॑	गग	रेरे	ग	गरे	—रे	स
डा	डिर	डिर	डिर	डा	रडा	डर	डा
नि़	ध़ध़	नि़	रे	—रे	रे	ग	रेरे
डा	डिर	डा	डा	डर	डा	डा	डिर
ग	प	—प	म॑	रे	गग	नि	रे
डा	डा	डर	डा	डा	डिर	डा	रा

1. Collection of Late Birendra Kishore Roy Chaudhuri.

Razakhani Gat of Raag Goud Sarang in Teen Tal.[1]

स्थायी

स	नि़	रे	स	ग	रे	म	ग
डा	रा	डा	रा	डा	रा	डा	रा
ग	मम	पमं	धप	रे	रेनि	–नि	स
डा	डिर	डिर	डिर	डा	रडा	डर	डा

अन्तरा

म	पप	पप	सं	–	रे	सं	नि
डा	डिर	डिर	डा	–	डा	डा	रा
ग	मम	पर्म	धप	रे–	रेनि	–नि	सा
डा	डिरि	डिर	डिर	डा	रडा	र	डा

1. Composed by Ustad Ashiq Ali Khan.

Maseetkhani Gat of Raag Bihag in Teen Tal.[1]

स्थायी

–	–	–	सनि		स	गमरेग	प	नि
पनिस	निध	प	पम		गम	गम	गपम	प
गम	गरे	सा	S					

मंझा

–	–	–	गपमप		गम	गरे	निरेसऩिस	ऩि
मप	ऩिऩि	स	स		ग	मग	गप	मप
गम	ग-	रेस	–					

अन्तरा

–	–	–	पम		गम	गम	प	नि
सं	सं	सं	सनिरेस		नि	पम	प	नि
सं	गरे	गंगं	सं		पम	गम	रेग	गपमप
गम	गरे	सा	–					

1. Composed by Late Shri Birendra Kishore Roy Chaudhuri. Collection of Dr. Sharmistha Sen.

राग देश , तीन ताल

स्थायी

	2	0	3
	रेरे	मम गS गरे गस	रेरे म पप नी नी
	डिर डिर	डा रडा रडा डिर	डा डिर डा रा
सं – प घ	म ग		
डा – डा रा	डा रा		

अन्तरा

	2	0	3
	रेरे मम	गS गरे गस रेरे	मS पप नी नी
	डिर डिर	डा रडा रडा डिर	डा डिर डा रा
सं – – प	म प नी सं	रे गंगं रेंरें मंमं	गं Sग निS निसं
डा – – डा	डा रा डा रा	डा डिर डिर डिर	डा डर डा रडा
पप म प नी	सं रें नी घ	प घ मप घप	म मग ग रे
डिरडा रा डा	रा डा रा डा	डा डा डिर डिर	डा रडा डर डार
रें – रे मप	घनी घप		
डा – डा डिर	डिर डिर		

1. Composed by Ustad Mushtaq Ali Khan

Composed by Dulhe Khan the son-in law of Feroj Khan (Adarang)

महादेव हे द्रेवता त्रिया भैरवी संग
शरतचंद्र की रैनसम भैरव उज्ज्वल अंग
भैरव राग भैरवी रागनी और नारी सुनि लेंही बरारी
मधुमाद सैंघवी बंगाली पाँच नारी संग रहे जुवाली इति शिवमतम
भैरवी विभावरी अरू तीजे गिन गुजरी को चौथी गुणकली
और बिलावल सुनारि है
पुत्र इनके सुनो भैरवी को देवगंधार ताकौ
सुघराई सौ अधिक पियार है
दूजै विभावरी अरू पुत्र है विभास वाको सूही को
विभास गन राखत संवार है तीजै सुन गुजरी को
पुत्र देवसाग भयो रागनि के वागवेल जूही निहारी है
चौथै गुगकली पुत्र वाकौ गंधार सुनौ कुरंक रागिनी
तो वाके मन की पियारी है पाँचे विलावल पुत्र वाकौ
सूहा सुन सूहे की पियारी नारी बहुली नियारी है ।

1. Sudarshan Acharaya , 'Sangeet Sudarshan,' p. 44.

CONCLUSION

Music with the universal appeal and potentiality to enlighten and ennoble is as old as life on earth. Music has universal appeal. The Indian Music enlightens soul to realise purpose and value of life. It is used for eliciting modes of detachment from the life of senses; to bring mass spiritual ecstasy, it is loved by the beasts and the birds; it is used by hunters, snakes charmers, labourers and farmers etc. Like in every old Indian art literature religion schooling, teaching emphasis was laid on self realisation; the union of the individual spirit with the supreme spirit the same emphasis must have been laid while Indian Music and raga system was evolved. The Indian Music is vibrations at a particular frequency and in a certain order rhythm and style. The same vibrations at the same frequency can be intolerable noise if produced in slightly wrong order. The Indian music is one whose frequency and vibrations when in order can raise to spiritual ecstasy; absorb a listener in *Smadhi*; force rains to come; burn; charm wildest elephants, beasts and snakes alike. Its frequency and vibrations seem to be very near or same to that of 'OM' the one word Brahma and its evolution is traced to Nad-Brahma. Its knowledge is Brahmajnana.

Indian Classical Music is much commercialised and corrupted now and we do not have musician like old masters. The old legends sound like fantasies. There are certain written facts in last one Century which gives sufficient proof of the facts what Indian Music is capable of doing. Sri Ramkrishna Paramahansadev, when he went to Varanasi on pilgrimage, listened to the Veena of Mahesh Sarkar and was absorbed in "Samadhi. The late Ustad

Mohammad Ali Khan the descendant of Tansen, when challenged in 1928 to play Deepak Raga performed it on a Rabab in the temple of Hanuman at Gaya and the flames evoked by the Deepak Raga burnt part of the musical instrument, which has been preserved in the temple and is still worshipped. The late Ustad Zakir-ud-din Khan of Udaipur at the first music conference in Baroda in 1916, when sang Megha Raga, a sudden storm brewed as the singing progressed, the rains poured in torrents and the disturbance lasted for a couple of hours. These anecdotes cannot be dismissed as idle gossip or old women's tales for modern and researches in sound waves have also testified to the power of a sound and its convertibility into energy.

The Indian Music developed earlier than in other countries. It was deeply associated with religion. Like Hindu religion its basis is scientific. From hymns which were chanted in the rituals during Vedic times it developed into classical form of music. In Natyashastra of Bharat, foundation of Indian music were well laid. When the Bhakti movement of Vallabha Sampradaya was in its full force and Caitanya, Meera, Tulsidasa, Guru Nanak, Swami Haridasa and Sufi's were there, *Dhrupada* was developed and finally brought to eminence by Raja Man Singh Tomar and his eminent court musicians like Nayaka Baksu, Nayaka Pandaviya, Mahmuda Lohanga and Nayaka Karna. It got appreciation, patronage and recognition by Akbar because of the presence of the great musician Tansen in his court. Akbar the great Mughal acclaimed Tansen as a greatest musician of India after the age of Bharat and history subsequently bears the fact that such a musician either was not born after Tansen till date. Sweet and repturous was his melody that it induced intoxication in some and sobriety in others. Tansen passed away on 26th April, 1586.

Although all may not be authentically known about Tansen, yet he has been enjoying as high esteem, appreciation and admiration as a musician, as Shakespeare and Tagore in literature, Ashoka amongst the rulers, Tulsidasa as poet of Hindi Literature and Kalidasa in

Sanskrit Literature. Tansen's date of birth and early life is completely unknown and musicologists have tried to prove one date or other. His becoming a Muslim cannot be also known. Saraswati Devi being his daughter and Misri Singh her husband historically cannot be proved, since it was 300 years after Tansen that Hakim Karam Imam wrote about Tansen's daughter.

Hindustani Music is indebted to Tansen, for the enriched, systematized and synthesized it in his times and added inventions and innovations to it. He raised Dhrupada as the highest expression of music. He reshaped the entire Dhrupada music by the addition of new ornamentations in *Meend, Gamaka* etc. which was lacking till that time. He examined, analysed 4000 Ragas & Raginis and discarded the bulk of them and retained only 400. He perfected the Indo-Muslim synthetic style of singing which later was known as *Darbari.* He composed about 1000 Dhrupadas some of which are still remembered for the wonderful exposition of the ragas and their very high poetic value which has special charms and emotional appeal. He created many ragas such as Darbari Kanara, Darbari Todi, Mian Ki Malhar, Mian Ki Sarang, Mian Ki Todi which are regarded up till now as the foremost ragas of Northern India. He has also written three books; Sangit Sara, Rag Mala and Sri Ganeshastotra.

The other indirect contribution to Indian Music by Tansen is *Gharana System* . Although in ancient times Gharana system existed under different names but only after Tansen. Gharana system got evolved. Senia Gharana was the first in this system and all Gharanas are off shots of this main Gharana. The Senia Gharana traditions established and followed in music by direct descendants of Tansen who received training under him adopted the unique style of singing of Dhrupada and playing instrumental music of Tansen tradition having enriched, modified and invented new styles of singing and new instruments after Tansen till today. Genealogical tree charts are drawn to trace the line of Bilas Khan and Misri Singh down to the present day musicians. No old reference is available mentioning Misri Singh or Saraswati Devi. The oldest author to have mentioned and written about Tansen's daughter was Hakim Karam Imam who wrote his book in 1855 about three Centuries after Tansen. Also many present authors have mentioned Rahim Sen as son of Masit Khan but actually Rahim Sen was son of Sukh Sen and was a descendant of Bilas Khan while Masit Khan was descendent of Misri Singh. All musicians who presently claim to be descendants of Bilas Khan would have been actually descendents of Misri Singh and Bilas Khan's line would not have been possible to trace after Rajras Khan had Rahim Sen been son of Masit Khan. The mix up between these two line has been because Misri Singh also became a Mohammadan and took to Rabab also. The inter marriages among the descendants; families having no fixed surnames and a gap of 200 years between the authors Faqirullah and next book on musicians by Hakim Karam Imam have resulted in much of the confusion. However genealogical tree chart is drawn from all the possible references available.

All senia Musicians till end of last Century whether Vocalist or Instrumentalists were Dhrupada singers. They encouraged Been, Rabab among old instruments, invented new instruments like Sur-Bahar and Sur-Sringer developed Sitar and in Vocal developed Khayal but they were all Dhrupada Singers, Sadarang who invented new form of singing Khayal; which presently is most famous never sang Khayal himself in the court. He made Been as solo instrument and sang only Dhrupada. His brother Khusroo Khan who developed Sitar played Sitar and Been but he too was a Dhrupada Singer. Great instrumentalist in Senia Gharana till end of 19th century like Niyamat Khan, Khusroo Khan, Masit Khan, Jafar Khan, Pyar Khan, Basat Khan, Rahim Sen, Amrit Sen, Bahadur Hussain Khan, Amir Khan, Gulam Mohammad Khan, Umrao Khan, Shokat Ali Khan, Wazir Khan and Dabir Khan etc. were very good Dhrupada singers. Some of them seldom gave Dhrupada performance in public. Rahim Sen had advised his son Amrit Sen not to play anything except Sitar but he had rigorous training initially in Dhrupada. Haidar Baksh Khan who died in later part of 19th Century at the age of 106 years, died moments after explaining about a Dhrupada to his one son. Here it can be inferred that Dhrupada was the basic of all Senia training in Indian Music. Developments and enrichment of present music whether instrumental or Vocal has been through Dhrupada singers. If in twentieth Century we have found no new invention or innovation in instrumental music or in vocal Music although all scientific and manufacturing facilities of the highest order are available can be inferred because present Senia musicians do not have any training in Dhrupada. Dhrupada can be said to be the seed of all developments in Indian Classical Music after Tansen. Presently there is no Senia worth name who may be said to be a Dhrupada singer.

By about eighteenth Century when Dhrupada became stereotyped and effete, a simplified derivation of it emerged in the form of Khayal. Khayal was in existence long before the style was popularized. Some scholars believe that Khayal singing was an offshot of the Qawali and others believe that Amir Khusro the great poet musician of the 13th century helped to popularise the Khayal style. In the 15th Century, the Sharqui rulers, who were fine petrons of the all arts, promoted Khayal singing, but then for the next few Centuries, though it was in use, it did not have the prestige and importance of the Dhrupada style in the royal courts. During the period of Muhammad Shah Rangeelay, Niyamat Khan (Sadarang) who had an enormous musical knowledge, brought Khayal to its highest popularity and respect. From his time to the present, it has been of an attraction equal to Dhrupada, and today it is the predominant style in our Classical Music. Sadarang himself composed thousands of Khayal songs in almost all the different ragas that are still sung with much ardour. Although Khayal became so popular but Senia's never sang it, even Sadarang being a good composer and developer of Khayal style himself never sang Khayal. Niyamat Khan founded the famous Kawwal Gharana through his disciples.

Rabab was introduced to Hindustani Music around the 14th Century and formely was a very popular folk instrument of North India. The instrument gained popularity from the time of Tansen and became a stylised Classical Instrument. Some musicologists believe that Tansen is credited to have invented Rabab. However Tansen was known as the best Rabab player and is responsible for raising it to the status of a classical instrument Tansen's descendants through his sons kept up the tradition by playing Rabab only for its sanctified or distinguished association with Tansen. After Niyamat Khan his descendants were very good Been and Rabab players. Famous exponents in Tansen's line were Chharju Khan, Jafar Khan, Pyar Khan Basat Khan, Nirmal Shah, Kasim Ali, Sadiq Ali Khan, Bahadur Hussain Khan, Ali Mohammad Khan and Mohammad Ali Khan. Mohammad Ali Khan was the last descendant of Tansen to have played Rabab. Most of the modern musicians are hardly acquainted with Rabab which has become almost extinct today. The main reason of its disappearance being that in rainy season its tuning was difficult and it would not emit good tones. Because of this problem. Jafar Khan and Gulam Mohammad Khan of Senia Gharana invented Sur-Sringar and Sur-Bahar. The both instruments were popularized by the Senia's with their creativity and imagination.

With the passage of time the Senia Gharana's specialities in various fields of music have been or are heading towards vanishing point except in Sitar. It is said to have got evolved from the earliest instruments during the time of Amir Khusroo. Khusroo Khan the younger brother of Niyamat Khan is credited with having invented the Sitar of six strings. Anything in music which is untraceable has been traced to Amir Khusroo it seems Khusroo Khan having the same name has been robbed by the musicologists of his invention. However gradually the developments in Sitar were brought by Senia's after Khusroo Khan. Masit Khan his grandson invented Masit Khani Baj which is very popular now-a-days. The Sitar in its shape and form owes much of the pioneering work done by Masit Khan. Rahim Sen popularised the Sitar further. Rahim Sen and his son Amrit Sen played Sitar so beautifully that their melody resulted in the death of other instuments. Sitar at present is most popular instrument of India. Everybody is well acquainted with the name and the form of this instrument. The structure and quality of the sound of the Sitar of today is the result of many years of research by Senia's which has improved its form and sound beyond recognition of what it originally was. In Drupada, Been, Rabab, Sur-Sringar, and Sur-Bahar deviating from Senia traditions are in vogue. In Sitar only Senia traditions are sustained and also enriched by some of the great musicians such as Ustad Mushtaq Ali Khan, Prof. Debu Chaudhuri, Pandit Ravi Shankar and Shri Nikhil Banarjee etc.

The story of Indian Music is interesting from earliest times to present day, it has great achievements to its credit. All of them can not be described in this book. There is necessity for more such ventures to put before the people the glorious achievements of India in the field of music for which sustained work will prove refreshingly rewarding and will revive Dhrupada Been, Rabab, Sur-Sringar and Sur-Bahar etc.

BIBLIOGRAPHY

1. Abul Fazal — AIN-I-AKBARI, English Translation by H.Blochmann, New Imperial Book Depot, New Delhi, 1st Edition, 1871, IInd Edition, 1965.
2. Abul Fazal — Akbarnama 3 Volumes, Volume II, III, Translation by H.Beveridge, Ess Ess Publication, Delhi,1972,1973.
3. Adil Shah — Kitab-I-Nauras of Ibrahim Adilashah II Edited by Nazir Ahmed, Bhartiya Kala Kendra, New Delhi,1956
4. Al-Badaoni — Muntakhbu-I-Twarikh, Abdul-Qadir/ibn-I-Muluk Shah known as AlBadaoni, 2 Vols., Ist Volume Edited by Ranking, IInd Volume Edited by Love, Academica Asiatica, Patna , India, 1973.
5 Anderson Otto — The bowed, Harp London,1930.
6. Ali.R. Nawab — Maarifun-Naghmat, Sangeet Karyalaya Hathras, Second Edition, 1958.
7. Ahobala — Sangeet Rarijat, Calcutta, 1884.
8 Acharya Brahaspati — Sangeet Chintamani, Sangita Karyalaya, Hathras, 1966.
9. Acharya Brahaspati — Musalmana Aur Bhartiya Sangeet, Rajkamal Prakashan, Delhi,1974.
10. Acharya Brahaspati — Dhrupada Aur Uska Vikas, Bihar Rashtrabhasha Parishad,1951.
11. Ahmed Najma Parveen — Hindustani Music, Published Ramesh Jain Manohar, New Delhi,1984.
12. Ahmed K.N. — Tabquat-E-Akbari, 3 Volumes, Calcutta, 1913,1927,1931,
13. Aggarwal V.K. — Trends and Traditions.
14. Akbar Darbar's — Hindi Poet Thesis Published by Lucknow University.
15. Bagchi P.C. — India and China, IInd Edition, New York.
16. Bharta-Natyashastra — Vol. II, Translation by Manohar Ghosh, Asiatic Society , Calcutta, 1961.
17. Bhatkhande Vishnu Narayan — Comparative Study of some of the leading music systems of the 15th, 16th, 17th, & 18th Centuries.
18. Bhava Bhatt — Anup Sangeet Ankush Bombay, 1916.
19. Bhatkhande,V.N. — A short historical survey of the music of Upper India, published by Karkhoro, Maneek Ji. Bombay, Samachar 1917. Reprint of a paper read at the All India Music Conference at Baroda, 1916.

20. Bhatkhande,V.N. — Hindustan Sangit Padhati, Hathras, 1962, Part IV 1957, 5 Volumes.
21. Bhatkhande, V.N. — Kramik Pustak Malika, 5 Volumes, Hathras.
22. Collection of Nayak Bakshu — Dhrupada by Edited Prem Lata Sharma, Sangeet Natak Academy, New Delhi, 1972.
23. Chaturdevi, Narmdeshwar — Kavi Tansen Aur Unka Kavya.
24. Chaturvedi, Narmdeshwar — Sangeetaghya Kaviyoon Ki Hindi Rachanaein; Sahitya Bhavan Ltd. Allahabd, 1955.
25. Chobey, Sushil Kumar — Sangeet Ke Gharanoo Ki Charcha, U.P. Hindi Granth Academy, Lucknow, 1977.
26. Caland — Introduction to Panchvamsha, Brahman Calcutta, 1931, Chapter II.
27. Captain Willard, N.A. — A Treatise on Music of Hindustan, Calcutta, 1834.
28. Damodar Chatur — Sangeet Darpan, Edited by K. Vasudeva Shastri, Tanjore,1952.
29. Deva B. Chaitanya — Indian Music, Published by Indian Music for Cultural Relations, 1974.
30. Deva B.C. — Musical Instruments, National Book Trust of India, 1977.
31. Dixit K.N. — Pre historic Civilization of Indus Valley.
32. Dutta B.N. — Indian Art in Relation to Culture, Calcutta 1956.
33. Dutta R.C. — (a) A History of Civilization in Ancient India, Volumes I-III.
34. Dutta R.C. — (b) The Epics and lays of ancient India, Calcutta, 1903.
35. Dvivedi — Gwalior Ke Tomartha, Vidya Mandir Prakashan Murar, Gwalior, 1976.
36. Dvivedi Hari — Maan Singh Aur Maan Kutuhal Gwalior.
37. Danielou Alain — (1) Introduction to the study of Musical Scales, London Indian Society, 1943.
(2) Northern Indian Music, Vol. I & II, London Unesco, 1954.
(3) Ragas of North Indian Music, London , Barrie and Rockliff, 1968,
38. Dattilam — A compendium of Ancient Indian Music, Lieden, E.J. Brill, 1970.
39. Day C.R. — Music and Musical Instruments of Southern India and the Deccan London Ademn. and Charles, 1891.
40. Dutta Bhupendranath — Indian Art in Relation to Culture Calcutta Ist Edition. 1956.
41. Dowsen John. — The History of India as told by its own historians—The Mohammadan Period, London, 1875.

42.	Faqirullah	Raag Darpan, A Persian Translation of Maan Kutuhala of Maan Singh Tomar, Translation into Persian by Faqirullah, with the title of Raga Darpana and Raga Darpana is translated into Hindi by H. Dvivedi with the title of Maan Singh Aur Maan Kutuhal, Gwalior reprint, 1956.
43.	Farmer H.G.	(1) History of Arabian Music London, 1929. (2) The Arabian Influence on Musical Theory. (3) The Music and the Musical Instruments of the Arabs.
44.	Faqeerullah Amir	Raag Darpan Manuscript by Dr. Zakir Hussain Library, Jamia Millia, New Delhi.
45.	Fox strangways	A.H. Music of Hindustan Oxford, Clarendon Press, 1965.
46.	Goswami O .	Story of Indian Music, Bombay, Asia Publishing, 1957,
47.	Gangoly O.C.	Ragas and Raganies Bombay, Nalanda Publication, 1948.
48.	Garg D.N.	Nibandha Sangeet, Sangeet Karyalaya Hathras, 1978.
49.	Gossain Chuni Lal Ji	Nada Vinoda Hindi, Banaras, 1896.
50.	Ghose, Isan Chandra	The Guptila Jataka (Translation into Bengali).
51.	Ghanashyamdasa	Sangit Sara Samgraha (Edition with introduction by Swami Prajanananda Ram Krishna), Vedanta Math, Calcutta, 1956.
52.	Goswami Pannalal	Nad Vinode Granth Narayandasa Jangalimala, Delhi, 1896.
53.	Krsnananda Vyas	Raag Kalpadrum in Bengali and Hindi Script Calcutta, 1842.
54.	Kothari, K.S.	Indian Folk Musical Instruments, New Delhi, Sangeet Natak Academy, 1968.
55.	Kaufmann Walter	Ragas of North India Calcutta Oxford, I.B.H., Publication, 1968.
56.	Kumbhakarna	Sangeet Raja, Vol. I, Banaras Univeristy, 1963.
57.	Krishan Swamy S.	Musical Instruments of Indian Delhi Publications Divisions, Govt. Of India, 1965.
58.	Karam Imam	Madunul Mausiqui, 1855.
59.	Macdonell, A.	India's Past— A Survey of her Literature Religious Languages and Antiquities, London 1956, Edited by K, Sambasine Shastri.
60.	Matanga Muni	Brihhadesi (Trivandrum Sanskrit Series, 1928.).
61.	Mangesh Ram Krishna	Sangit Makranda of Narda, Teleng, Baroda, 1920.
62.	Mukherjee D.P.	Indian Music an Introduction Bombay, Kulab Publication 1945.
63.	Mitra R . L.	The Taittiriya Brahmana Calcutta, 1855.

64. Mukhopadhyaya Sri Hari Narayan — Dhrupada Swarlipi, Part I, Indian Press Ltd. Prayag, 1929.
65. Mitra Rajendra Lal — Indo Aryan, Vol. I & II, Calcutta, 1950.
66. Mukherjee Dr. Kumud — Hindu Civilization (2nd Edition, 1950.)
67. Mani Ram Ustad — Sitar - Darpan,
68. Miraat-E-Aftabnuma, — India Office Library, London, Reza Library, Rampur.
69. Mittal — Sangeet Samrat Tansen, Jivani Aur Rachnaean, Sahitya Sansthan, Mathura, 1960.
70. Narada — Sangit Makranda, Baroda, 1920.
71. Narada — Nardiya Shikshya, Samveda (with Shiksha Vivarna commentary of Shri Bhatla Shubhakara) Banaras Sanskrit Series, 1893, Mysore 1946.
72. Nizami K.H. — Purani Delhi Ke Halaat, Translation of Dargah Quli Khan.
73. Prajanananda — A Historical Study of Indian Music, Anandhara Prakashan, Calcutta, 1965.
74. Prajanananda — Music of the Nations (A Comparative Study) Munshi Ram Manohar Lal, 1973.
75. Prajanananda — Historical Development of Indian Music, Calcutta, Firma, K.L. Mukhopadhyay, 1960.
76. Popley, H.A. — Music of India, Calcutta, Y.M.C.A. Publishing House,Second Edition , 1950.
77. Pandit Ravi Shankar — My Music My Life,Bombay Vikas Publication, 1967.
78. Parameshwara — (1) Vina Lakshana (Baroda, 1959), (2) Vina Prapathaka (Baroda 1959).
79. Pundrika Vithala — Sadraga-Chandrodya, Bombay (Early 20th Century)
80. Parshva Deva — Sangita Samaya Sara (Trivandrum Sanskrit Series, 1925).
81. Roy Chaudhuri Birendra Kishore — Indian Music & Mian Tansen Gouripur, Music Trust, Calcuttta.
82. Rogers and Beveridge — Memories of Jahangir, Vol.I.
83. Rosenthal Ethel — Story of Indian Music and its Instruments, New Delhi, Oriental Book, Reprint Corporatioin, 1970.
84. Ranade G.H. — Hindustani Music, Arya Bhushan Press, Poona, 1939.
85. Ranade G.S. — Hindustani Music and Outlines of its Physics and Aesthetics Bombay, Popular Prakashan, 1971.
86. Roy Chaudhuri Bimal Kant — Bhartiya Sangeet Kosh, Calcutta.
87. Rasik I.K. — Risala-E-Zikre - Mughannian-E- Hindustan, Edited by S. Haider, Department of Arabic and Persian, Patna University, 1961.
88. Sach Curt — The History of Musical Instruments, New York.

89. Sahukar, Mani — Indian Classical Music, Reliance Publishing House, New Delhi-8, 1986.
90. Sangeet Kala Vihar — English Suppliement Nos. 3 and 4, Baroda Hira Lal Kapadia Jain Data about Musical Instruments.
91. Sarkar S.C — Some aspects of the earliest Social History of India, London 1928.
92. Sharangdeva — Sangit Ratnakara Vols. I, II & III, Adyar Series.
93. Subbaro T.V. — Studies in Indian Music Bombay, Asia Publishing House, 1965.
94. Sahasrasa — A Collection of Nayak Bakshu's Dhrupada, Edited by Prem Lata Sharma, Sangeet Natak Academy, New Delhi, 1972.
95. Sanyal A.N. — Ragas and Raginies Orient Layman's, 1959.
96. Srivastava Indurama — Dhrupada, Published Moti Lal Banarsidas, 1980.
97. Somesvara,Mansollasa — Vol. III, Edited by G.K. Shringodekar, Gaekwards Oriental Series No. 28, Baroda, 1961.
98. Sudarshan Acharya — Sangeet Sudarshan, Published in 1915.
99. Sharma, B. — Bhartiya Sangeet Ka Itihas, Sangeet Karalaya, Hathras.
100. Sulochna and Brahaspati — Khayal Sangeet, July, 1979.
101. Sambamoorthy.P. — Catalogue of Musical Instruments exhibited in Government Museum, Madras, Govt. of Madaras 1962.
102. Shastri, Hari Prasad — The Ramayana of Valmiki, London, 1957.
103. Thakur Jai Dev Singh — The Evolution of Khayal Commemoration, Volume in Honour of Dr. S.N.Ratnajankar, 1961.
104. Tansen Samaroh Gwalior M.P. Govt.Publication, Shakobad.1889.
105. Tagore S.M. — Universal History of Music, Calcutta, 1896.
106. Tohfat-Ul-Hind, — Edited by N.H. Ansari Published in Iran 1950.
107. Usulun- Naghat-e - Asifi, — Dr. Zakir Hussain Library Jamia Millia Islamia, New Delhi.
108. Ustad Villayat Husain Khan — Sangitayoon Ke Sansmaran, Sangit Natak Academi.
109. Vasant — Sangit Visharad.

JOURNALS, ARTICLES AND MANUSCRIPTS

1. Acharya Brahaspati, Article Qawwali Ek Bhartiya Shaili, January-February, 1979.
2. Acharya Brahaspati, Bhartiya Sangeet Ke Param Bhakht Sangeet Article, April, 1968.
3. Acharya Brahaspati, Musalman, Ghazal,Qawwali Aur Khayal, Sangeet January-February, 1976.
4. Archaeological Survey of India, 1959, Bulletin No 15.
5. Arshi, I.A. Hindustan Ke Chand Mashhoor Mausiquaar, Article Aaj-Kal, August 1956.
6. Arshi, I.A. Nadirat-e-Shahi, Edited Raza Library Rampur.
7. Chaudhuri Birendra Kishore, Revival of Dhrupada Lakshya Sangeet Article in English September, 1958.
8. Ginde, K.R. Article in Hindi Dhrupada Lakshya Sangeet March, 1957.
9. Mutatkar Sumati, Evolution of Indian Music (A series of Special Articles and papers read at the symposium arranged by All India Radio).
10. Matatkar Sumati Some Aspects of Dhrupada illustrated Talk.
11. Sharma K. Thumri Udgam Aur Vikas Sangeet Kala Vihar August, 1956.
12. Singh S.B. Khayali Duniya Ki Upaj Khayal Sangeet Article, May, 1965.
13. Shukla Shatrughan Khayal Ek Punarvalokan Sangeet, January-February. 1976.
14. Journal of the Music Academy, Madras.
15. Journal of the Sangeet Natak Academy, New Delhi.
16. Sangeet No 10, Sangeet Karyalaya, Hathras.
17. Sangeet Kala Vihar, English Supplement Nos. 3 and 4, Baroda.
18. A Monograph on Music Vols. I & II.
19. Archaeological Survey of India, 1959, Bulletin No. 15.
20. Usulun-Naghmat-e-Asifi, Dr. Zakir Hussain Library Jamia Millia Islamia, New Delhi.